# FROM *Girls* TO Grrrlz

## A HISTORY OF ♀ COMICS FROM TEENS TO ZINES

TRINA ROBBINS

CHRONICLE BOOKS

SAN FRANCISCO

## Dedication

This book is dedicated to my big sister, Harriet, whose *Patsy Walker* comics, devoured by me at an impressionable age, started me on the rocky road to my so-called career in comics.

## Acknowledgments

This would not have been much of a book without help from the following people, in no particular order: Paul Curtis, Michelle Nolan, Robert Beerbohm, the Flying Leialoha Brothers, John Workman, Paul Castiglia, Heather Cassell, Joe Simon, Joe Edwards, Dan DeCarlo, Stan Lee, George Gladir, Steven Rowe, Barb Rausch, Robin Morgan, Ann Forfreedom, Laura X, Susan Brownmiller, Alta, Alice Molloy, Elayne Wexler-Chaput, Naomi Basner, Martha Thomases, and Bonnie Eisenberg. Thank you all!

Thanks also to Randall W. Scott for creating the index.

Text copyright © 1999 by Trina Robbins.
All artwork reproduced herein copyright individual copyright holders. All rights reserved. No part of this book may be reproduced in any form without written permission from the publisher.

Library of Congress Cataloging-in-Publication Data:

Robbins, Trina
Girls to grrrlz : a history of women's comics from teens to zines / by Trina Robbins.
 p.     cm.

Includes index.
ISBN 0-8118-2199-4

1. Comic books, strips, etc.— United States—History and criticism. 2. Women—Comic books, strips, etc. I. Title.
PN6725.R58  1999
741.5'973'082—dc21
        98-24966
          CIP

Printed in Hong Kong.

Cover & book design by Martine Trélaün

Distributed in Canada by Raincoast Books
8680 Cambie Street
Vancouver, British Columbia
V6P 6M9

10 9 8 7 6 5 4 3 2 1

Chronicle Books
85 Second Street
San Francisco, California
94105

www.chroniclebooks.com

# Table of Contents

# Introduction

I'll never forget the day I discovered the world of *Love and Rockets*, produced by Jaime and Gilbert Hernandez. My boyfriend (now husband) Mark and I stopped by the local comic-book store so he could pick up the latest issues of *Weirdo* and *Neat Stuff*. I wasn't planning to buy any comic books. I wasn't into comics, hadn't been since sixth grade, when I'd been an avid reader of *Archie* and *Little Lotta*. Once I outgrew those comics, I was confronted by the realization that, besides those few titles that cater to very young girls, comics were actually a guy's medium. I loved *Betty and Veronica*, but as a teenager I wanted something a bit more dimensional, something I wouldn't find in these guy-laden shops filled with titles such as *X-Men* and *Spiderman*. Usually I declined to accompany Mark when he went for his comic fix.

So there I was, politely waiting on the sidelines inside the shop, self-consciously glancing around at nothing in particular, when suddenly a grimacing punk girl with blue and black choppy hair and a yellow scarf around her neck beckoned to me from the far side of the room. She was "Errata Stigmata," a cartoon on the cover of *Love and Rockets* no. 11. What was this? As I flipped through the fictional pages of grrrl rock musicians, a female champion wrestler, and young women with realistic postadolescent lives, I realized there was more to comic life than violent one-dimensional superhero stories, or one-page gags about dumping Reggie for Archie at the Choklit Shop. What a surprising delight it was to feast my eyes on characters I could relate to, characters who were drawn as spunky as the girls in *Archie* (in an updated, eighties, goth-punk style), but were engaged in much deeper, truer-to-life situations (the cover said "Recommended for Mature Readers"). I became instantly hooked on *L&R*, and desperately wondered: Were there other engaging comix about women? If so, how long has this type of graphic novel been around? Is there a subculture of female comic readers that I don't know about?

Finally, in *Girls to Grrrlz*, these questions are answered by girly grrrl Trina Robbins, and I can't think of a more qualified woman for the job. To write a book like *Girls to Grrrlz*, one needs to have a well-rounded appreciation for both the girls of comics (Katy Keene, Little Dot, Josie and the Pussycats, Betty and Veronica, etc.) and the grrrlz of comix (Bitchy Bitch, Hothead, Little Goth Girl, Maggie and Hopy, etc.). Trina is a veteran of each.

Trina was a riot grrrl before the term was coined. Like the grrrlz of the nineties who banded together to mark their territory in the male-dominated punk scene, Trina defied the exclusive boys' club of the comic-book world back in the sixties when she headed the first all-women comic book, called *It Ain't Me, Babe*. She then went on to cofound the Wimmen's Comix Collective, which put out the femme anthology *Wimmen's Comix* for over ten years. Trina linked arms with her artistic sisters and caused a riot in the underground comic scene. Never before had there been comics about women who explored issues such as homosexuality, orgasms, and abortion!

But Trina, like most women, isn't all grrrl. Everyone needs balance in their lives, and she shows us her softer, girlier side through her writing for and illustrations of characters such as Barbie, the Little Mermaid, Wonder Woman, and Betty Boop. Trina once told me in an interview, "It's total bullshit to say that girls don't read comics. Girls read comics when there are comics for girls to read." For anyone who doesn't believe this, as well as anyone with a general appreciation for comics, *Girls to Grrrlz* is an entertaining, nostalgic, as well as eye-opening account of girl characters and their effect on—as well as how they've been affected by—the comic-book world. And Trina, being a major part of this history, is the perfect person to tell the story.

—Carla Sinclair, author of *Net Chick*

# Chapter One
# Girls' Comics
## 1941–1957

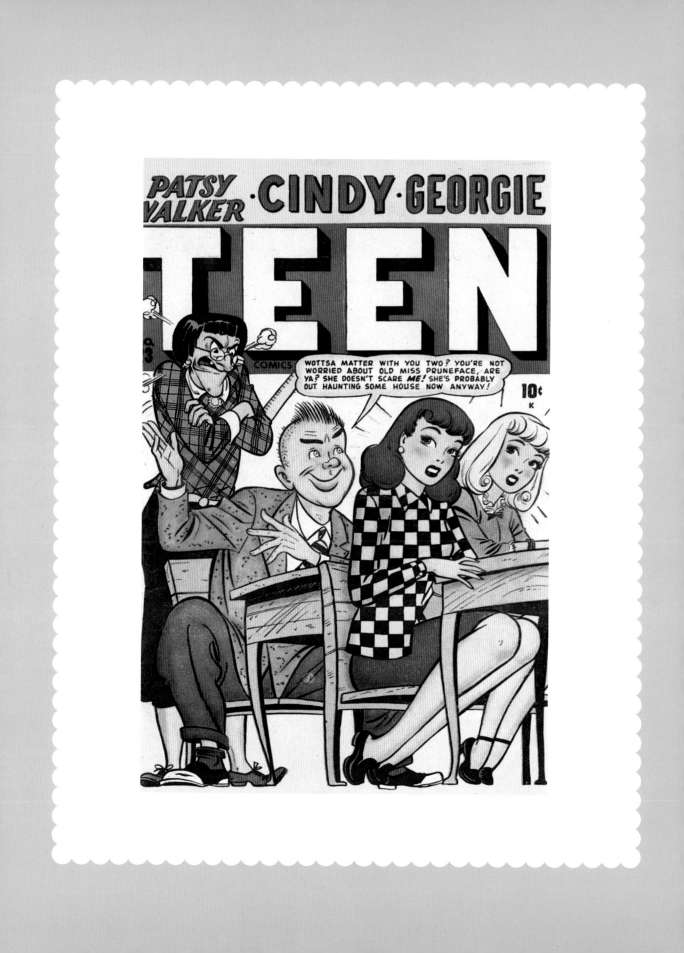

**WALK** into any comic-book store. A giant cutout of a superhero stands in the window, muscles bulging improbably, a grimace on his lantern-jawed face. Inside, the store is jam-packed with young males, some not so young. You'll have to look hard to find a girl. The boys are reading and buying comic books with covers that feature costumed and caped guys similar to the one in the window, or even more improbably breasted women attired in little besides thong bikinis and spike-heeled, thigh-high boots. If you're of the female persuasion, odds are you take one look at the scene before you, shrug, and decide you'd really rather read a novel.

It was not always thus.

Once there was a time when more girls than boys read comics, a time when comics for girls sold in the millions, outnumbering every other kind of comic book.

And it all started with *Archie*.

By 1941, the fledgling comic-book industry had been booming since 1938, when two teenage boys from Cleveland, Jerry Siegel and Joe Shuster, created *Superman*. Kids and adults had been reading comic strips in their daily and Sunday papers since the beginning of the century, but there was a distinct advantage to getting your comic story complete, between two covers. In those days, before television, comics provided a less expensive alternative to movies—they only cost a dime!—and they were disposable. You could roll up a comic book and stash it in your back pocket; better yet, you could conceal it in your loose-leaf notebook and read it beneath your desk during math class. But comic books, inundated with caped and costumed superheroes, served as entertainment for boys. Little existed in the way of comics aimed toward girls.

This, at least, was the situation in 1941 when John Goldwater, publisher of *Pep* comics, called two teenage boys, Joe Edwards and Bob Montana, into his office and asked them to design a new kind of comic character for him.

MLJ Publications, named for partners Maurice Coyne, Louis Silberkleit, and John Goldwater, had been publishing *Pep*, and other comics, for a year. Already these publications, with names like *The Shield*, *The Comet*, *The Rocket*, *The Black Hood*, and *Fireball*, had featured their share of superheroes, but the partners wanted something different. As Goldwater put it,

## "Why does every book have to be Superman?"

Along with editor Harry Shorten, Edwards and Montana set to work, bouncing ideas between them. What they came up with, Edwards remembers, was what, being young, they knew best: "chasing girls and not having enough money." The result was definitely not *Superman*.

Archie Andrews, his pal Jughead, and a wistful blond named Betty made their debut in issue no. 22 of *Pep*, dated December 1941, and for the next seventeen years, teen comics ruled the roost.

Montana and Edwards took their characters from real life. Another MLJ artist, Harry Lucy, had been dating a girl with a sister named Betty, so they used her name. They based Veronica on the gorgeous daughter of a rich man in Montana's hometown, Haverhill, Massachusetts. Much of *Archie*, in fact, came from Haverhill, including Archie's hangout, Pop's Choklit Shop.

Archie, 1950. Art by Bob Montana.

Pop's was based on an ice cream parlor called the Chocolate Shop, where Montana himself used to hang out doodling on napkins. Haverhill became Archie's hometown, Riverdale.

December 1941, the date of *Archie*'s birth, was also the month that America went to war. *Archie* was barely launched when first Montana, and then Edwards, got drafted. Goldwater and Shorten kept the strip afloat with artists like Bill Vigoda, Samm Schwartz, and Harry Sahle, all drawing in what we recognize today as the "*Archie* style," so that by the time Montana and Edwards returned in 1945, the red-headed teenager with waffle marks on his head had become a runaway success. He had been starring in his own book, *Archie*, since 1942, and also had a nationwide newspaper strip and weekly radio show to his credit. In 1946, MLJ Publications renamed themselves after their most famous character, becoming Archie Publications.

*Archie*'s success was a case of the right teenager at the right time. Superhero comics, which dominated the market during the war, had been steadily losing their audience. Perhaps the returning GIs, who had made up a large part of the comic-reading market, were now more interested in buying homes on the GI Bill and raising families, or perhaps the general public was tired of violence after almost five years of war. Whatever the reason, soon after

A 1952 ad for **Jughead**.

the war DC Comics' superhero line was reduced by more than half, and other companies followed suit. The departing superheroes left a gap on the newsstands that was quickly filled by horror comics, westerns, cartoon animals, "Crime Does Not Pay" titles—and teen comics aimed at girls. The new genres succeeded admirably, and the size of the comics industry doubled between 1946 and 1949. By the late 1940s, one in three periodicals sold in America was a comic book.

The concept of teenagers was still pretty new when *Archie* came along. In the last century and before, there had been no teenagers as we now know them. At the age of sixteen, typical boys were already working hard, and girls were married and raising families. It's important to remember that people didn't live all that long in those days, so if you were going to die of old age at fifty, you needed to start having babies at sixteen. Only during the twenties, when the country caught its collective breath after the First World War, did Americans have the leisure to experience teenhood. The first teen comic strips, like "Harold Teen" and "Etta Kett," appeared in newspapers in the twenties, followed in the thirties by a spate of teen movies starring the likes of Judy Garland, Mickey Rooney, and Deanna Durbin. The new teenagers jitterbugged and lindied to swing music played by big bands and swooned to the songs of Frank Sinatra. By the year of *Archie*'s origin, the teenager had become an established part of the American landscape, and *Archie*'s subtitle was "America's Typical Teenager."

Betty's rival, Veronica, had to wait for four more issues of *Pep* before she showed up, completing the eternal triangle. For more than half a century, Betty has loved Archie, who loves Veronica, who loves herself. Today the original copy of *Pep* no. 22 in good condition sells for more than fifteen hundred dollars.

Archie's sarcastic pal Jughead was next to get his own book, in 1949, and a year later Archie's girls, Betty and Veronica, got to fight over Archie in their own comic book.

*Betty and Veronica* eventually became the best-selling title in the *Archie* comics line.

Through its roughly sixty-year life span, all of Archie's best friends have at one time or another starred in their own titles. Aside from *Betty and Veronica*, Betty can boast of *Betty and Me*, *Betty's Diary*, and just plain *Betty*, while Veronica, for all her dough, has had only one solo book, called— what else?—*Veronica*. Some of Jughead's titles were pretty strange. Besides *Jughead's Jokes*, the skinny guy with the funny hat starred in *Jughead's Diner* and *Jughead's Time Police*. Even Archie's snide rich rival, Reggie, had *Reggie*, *Reggie and Me*, and *Reggie's Wise Guy Jokes* to call his own.

The majority of *Archie* readers were girls, ages six to thirteen. Demographics from within the past twenty-five years show that 60 percent of *Archie* readers are female and 40 percent male, and although there are no statistics from the earlier days, ads for feminine items like charm bracelets, handbags, belts, and even girdles—perhaps for the readers' mothers?—that ran in the *Archie* comic books of the 1940s and 1950s reflect the typical reader's gender.

While Joe Edwards and Bob Montana served in the army, new MLJ comic characters had joined *Archie* on the newsstands. Two dumb blonds, an Archie clone named Wilbur and a girl named Suzie, appeared in *Laugh Comix* in the summer of 1944, and within the year both had their own comics. *Wilbur* was exactly like *Archie*—obviously the publishers reasoned that if one wacky teenage boy

Wilbur, 1956.

The main characters from **Laugh Comix**, August 1955.

I'M GLAD MR. HACKBOTTOM SAW THINGS MY WAY! I DON'T THINK I WAS CUT OUT FOR THE TAXICAB BUSINESS, ANYHOW!

was a hit, two would be even better—with all the same characters under new names. Wilbur, like Archie, sported waffle marks on his head, only his Jughead was a red-haired woman-hater named Red. He even had blond and brunette girlfriends fighting over him. The two girls, Linda and Laurie, were named after Harry Shorten's daughters.

While Linda, Laurie, Betty, and Veronica were hardly role models for young girls, wasting as much time and energy as they did fighting over boys, at least they were bright, perky teenagers.

Suzie wasn't so great. She dressed up in nylons and high heels, and was

Two dumb blonds. Above left: Suzie; above right: Torchy.

definitely out of high school, but she couldn't hold a job. Her funny-looking boyfriend, Ferdie, was even dumber. But Suzie was a looker, and her comic book featured paper dolls and pinups of her posing in bathing suits or cute costumes.

Suzie, however, was positively wholesome compared to *Torchy*, published by Quality Comics in 1949 and 1950. Artists Bill Ward and Gill Fox put Torchy and her roommate, Tess, in six-inch spikes and nylons with seams down the back, and clingy dresses that exposed lots of cleavage. Like Suzie, Torchy was always looking for work, though she should have been able to earn a good living posing for pinups, Betty Page style. The "dumb blond" character was an unfortunate comic-book theme that kept popping up during the 1940s and 1950s, and is mercifully gone today.

Katy Keene, on the other hand, who made her first appearance in issue no. 5 of *Wilbur* comics, was a Betty Page look-alike, but the resemblance ended there. Katy Keene was no bimbo and she had a good job—she was a movie star. She also got her own comic book to star in by 1949. Bill Woggon drew her in a different style from the other comics in the *Archie* line, bestowing her with enormous eyes framed by thick, long lashes. Katy's comic books included puzzles, games, coloring pages, and even rebuses, along with short, simple, pleasant stories. But what endeared Katy to her many fans—and there *was* an active Katy Keene fan club—were the paper dolls in each issue. Paper dolls in comics were nothing new; even newspaper strips like "Blondie" had featured paper dolls as early as the 1920s. And reader-designed paper dolls had also been done before. But Woggon took the concept of reader participation to dizzying heights. Along with the many paper dolls in his comics, he added pinups and even horses, cars, and rocket ships designed by readers, and included photos of his young fans. In those pre-computer days, *Katy Keene* comics were as close as one could get to an interactive comic book. Woggon cheerfully credited fans' designs for Katy's poses, gag and story ideas, and even poetry. His relationship to his readers was up close and personal, and his comics often included photos of himself, sometimes wearing a cowboy outfit, folksy

I see by your outfit that you are a cowboy. "Boss Man" Bill Woggon, from **Katy Keene Annual**, 1955-56.

messages from him to his fans, and coupons for paper dolls that readers could clip out and send, along with a dime, to his "Woggon Wheels Ranch" address in Santa Barbara, California. The *Katy Keene* paper dolls represented all the supporting characters of the comic, including Katy's boyfriends, prizefighter KO Kelly and rich guy Randy Van Ronson. The paper doll designs often reflected each character's idiosyncrasies. Katy's movie star friend, Lucki Red, for instance, wore four-leaf-clover outfits or dresses decorated with a lucky seven, while Katy's little sister, Sis, the "Candy Kid," donned candy-cane dresses. Bertha, Katy's pleasingly plump friend, was fond of both cooking and eating, and usually had apron designs for her paper doll wardrobes.

Katy helps crippled children, from **Katy Keene Annual**, 1955-56.

At their peak in the 1950s, Katy Keene comics spawned their own mini-industry, with almost as many titles as the Archie comics: *Katy Keene Fashion Book Magazine*, *Katy Keene Holiday Fun*, *Katy Keene Pinup Parade*, *Katy Keene Annual*, *Katy Keene Spectacular*, *Katy Keene Charm*, *Katy Keene Glamour*, and *Katy Keene 3-D*. Among the many readers cutting out the paper dolls and mailing in clothing designs during this period were fashion designers Betsey Johnson, Willi Smith, Calvin Klein, and Anna Sui; illustrator Mel Odom; and Barbie artist Barb Rausch. So many little girls, and quite a few boys, cut out the paper doll and pinup pages of their favorite comic book that uncut copies of *Katy Keene* are scarce today, and buying one will set you back an arm and a leg.

Katy fought with her rich blond rival, Gloria Grandbilt, sometimes over juicy roles in movies, sometimes over boyfriends like rich boy Randy Van

**Katy** AND **Bertha** KITCHEN KUT-UPS

SENT IN BY KATY'S READERS

PRISCILLA JOHNSTON, 509 WEST 6TH ST. HOPE, ARK.

BY JOAN SWANSON, 22 SUYDAM ST. BROOKLYN 21, N.Y.

BY SHIRLEE VANDURERE, 3530 DUNN AVE., CHEYENNE, WYO.

SKIRT by PATRICIA IANNONE, 3326 IDELL ST., L.A., CALIF.

CHEF HAT + APRON by MAURINE GARDNER, STAR RT.1 CRANE, TEXAS

BY ROBERT JOHNSON, BOX #1 AVONDALE ORLANDO, FLA.

If you'd like to send for these 2 pin-up dolls of KATY and BERTHA with lots of cutouts to fit just clip out this TEA-POT and sign your name and address to tag and send it with 20¢ (in U.S. coin) 10¢ for each set to KATY KEENE WOGGON WHEELS RANCH SANTA BARBARA, CALIF.

TO KATY KEENE WOGGON WHEELS RANCH, SANTA BARBARA, CALIF. HERE IS MY 20¢ PLS. SEND ME THESE 2 SETS.

NAME _____ PRINT CLEARLY
ADDRESS _____
CITY _____ ZONE _____ STATE _____

BY CAROLYN McELWAIN P.O. BOX 567 RUSKIN, FLA.

SUGAR LUMP

BARB B.Q.    BARB I.Q.

CHOW CHOW

CHEF OUTFIT by NANCY W. DEVEN, 1 E LINCOLN KIMBERLY, WIS. (AGE ___)

SEND YOUR FASHION IDEAS FOR KATY, BERTHA AND THE WHOLE GANG TO KATY at WOGGON WHEELS RANCH, SANTA BARBARA, CALIFORNIA.

"Kitchen Kut-ups": paper dolls of Katy Keene and her chunky friend Bertha from 1955. Art by Bill Woggon, adapting readers' designs.

THE Archie DIGEST LIBRARY

**KATY KEENE**
Comics Digest Magazine
NO. 1
$1.35
06940 CMA

featuring
• FUN
• GAMES
• PIN-UPS
• FASHIONS
• ROMANCE
• CUT-OUTS
• ADVENTURE
AND MORE!

WE LOVE KATY!

PREMIERE COLLECTOR'S ISSUE

Katy Keene, 1986. Art by John Lucas.

Ronson or boxer KO Kelly, until she was canceled in 1961. But more than twenty years later, in 1983, pressure from her still active fan club inspired Archie Publications to come out with a four-issue reprint book, and then six more years of original Katy Keene comics. From 1984 until 1990, Katy's new regular artist was John Lucas, who had been a Katy Keene fan back in the late 1950s. John's father had worried about his seven-year-old son reading a "girl's comic," but the many rocket-tailfinned car designs sent in by boy fans and the photos of Woggon in a cowboy outfit reassured him.

A redhead named Ginger made her debut in the pages of Suzie comics in 1945, and graduated to her own title (subtitled "America's Typical Teen-age Girl") in 1951. Drawn by George Frese with wide cute-as-a-button eyes and an animated expression, Ginger was absolutely adorable. Frese further enlivened the comic by peppering it with speed lines, flying sweat drops, and little hearts popping up in the air around Ginger's head. The book's pages are in constant motion.

## Ginger had a habit of falling in love with her various high school teachers,

but she could—and did—take charge when necessary. In a story from the first issue, "The Bear Facts," she talks her father, Mr. Snapp, into taking her along on a hunting trip with his boss, B. J., but when B. J. aims his rifle at a rabbit, she pushes it aside. Ginger lectures him, while her father cowers: "You ought to be *ashamed!!* How do you know but that poor little thing might have been a *mama bunny?* Shame!" The two men make Ginger promise to mind her own business, but when they take aim at a Bambi-like deer, she frightens it off, shouting, "I hope you miss! I hope you miss!!", and then tells them, "I think it's *shameful* the way you men have to try to shoot the head off of every poor animal you see!" But when a gigantic bear attacks the hunting party, the men run for cover, and Ginger fights the bear off by whacking it on its nose with the butt of a rifle. She is compassionate enough to care about small, helpless creatures, but brave and resourceful enough to defend herself against a real threat.

Sadly, Ginger only lasted three years; in 1954, she was replaced by a much younger girl named Li'l Jinx, created by Joe Edwards after Harry Shorten suggested he come up with a little girl character. During the war,

Edwards had drawn a strip called "Private Jinx" for the army papers, so he took that name for his mischievous new character, basing her adventures on those of his own kids. Li'l Jinx fared better than Ginger, lasting well into the 1970s.

Li'l Jinx was only one of many cute little girl characters in comics, usually with the word *Little* or *Li'l* before their names. Harvey Comics published three of them, starting with *Little Audrey* in 1952, followed by *Little Dot* in

Ginger, characteristically in love with her teacher, from **Ginger** no.1, 1951.

1953, and *Little Lotta* in 1955. Each girl had an obsession: Little Dot with polka dots, and Little Lotta was obsessed with food—there was a *lotta* Little Lotta. By the sixties, all three little girls could be seen on Sunday morning television in the form of animated cartoons. Their books lasted until the mid-1970s, and were all brought back again in 1992.

The queen—or princess—of all the "little" characters was Little Lulu, whose comic books started in 1945. The smart little moppet (that was her name: Lulu Moppet!) was the brainchild of Marge Henderson Buell, who drew her for the *Saturday Evening Post* from 1935 through 1944. Although Henderson Buell retained the rights to her corkscrew-curled creation until 1971, she never drew the comic books. These were mostly the work of the brilliant and talented John Stanley, with help from Irving Tripp and Arnold Drake. Although Lulu was already a clever kid in her early *Saturday Evening Post* cartoons, Stanley fleshed the character out further and added story lines that continued from issue to issue. One was the theme of Lulu's tubby little friend, Tubby, who disguised himself as a detective called The Spider and stopped at nothing in his attempts to prove that Lulu's father, the mild-mannered Mr. Moppet, was a master criminal. Others were tales within tales, created when Lulu made up stories to tell Alvin, the little boy she baby-sat. The heroine of Lulu's stories was always Lulu herself, playing the part of a poor little orphan with patches on her dress. The "poor little girl" had a way of getting lost in the forest while picking "beebleberries," and running afoul of Witch Hazel, who constantly cackled

Li'l Jinx.

("cackle,

and, in later issues, the witch's niece, Little Itch, who cickled ("cickle cickle!").

A third story line in *Little Lulu* involved the boys' clubhouse, an upended wooden crate

bearing the hand-lettered sign, "No Girls Allowed." Lulu and her friend Annie were forever devising ways to get into the boys' club, while Tubby and his friends tried to keep them out. Somehow, even though Lulu never succeeded in crashing the club, she always won anyway.

# cackle!")

In a 1951 story, Lulu empties her piggybank to buy a stuffed owl that Tubby and the boys want for their clubhouse. She gives it to them on the condition that they let her join their club. The boys hatch a plot: "You can be a member, Lulu, for as long as we have that **OWL**!" As soon as Lulu leaves, they hide

A gallery of "Littles": Little Lotta, Little Lulu, Little Dot, and Little Audrey.

A fashion page drawn by Christopher Rule,

the owl in the woods behind their clubhouse. She returns, only to hear that the owl has been stolen and her club membership is now history. Poor Lulu sadly wanders off into the woods and finds the owl in the bushes where the boys had hidden it. "Oboy! What luck!" she exclaims. "Somebody must have hidden it here after they stole it!" She returns the owl to the dismayed boys, who get her out of the way by sending her off on an errand. This time they decide to hide the owl where no one can find it, at the top of the biggest tree in the woods. Reaching the designated hiding place isn't easy for the little guys, who must climb on top of each other to get there, and they're plumb tuckered out after their ordeal. But, as one of the boys says, "Well, the owl is safe, anyway."

Cut to Lulu, walking through the woods after her errand. As she passes the tree, crows dislodge the owl, and it falls to her feet. Lulu sees the light: "Something tells me I'm out of the club again." Leaving the owl outside, she enters the clubhouse, and is told, "Somebody stole the owl again while you were away! You are no longer a member of this club!" That's okay with Lulu, who walks out, saying, "I don't want to belong to a **BOY'S** club anyway!" She returns the owl, getting back her money. The last panel shows the unsuspecting boys climbing on top of each other again to reach the treetop. "I hate to think of climbin' that tree again, but it's worth it to get that owl," they say. "We sure put one over on Lulu!"

Variations on the boys' club theme would be repeated in girls' comics through the years. *Little Lulu* stayed in print for more than forty years, entertaining and inspiring at least four generations of girls.

The runaway success of *Archie* opened up a vast market for teen comics. During the 1940s and 1950s, titles by publishers cashing in on *Archie*'s success sprang up like mushrooms after the rain. The many teen comics that followed in the footsteps of "America's Typical Teenager" all nominated their

The teenage superheroine gets herself out of a jam, from **Miss America** no.4, 1945. Art by Pauline Loth.

own characters as America's "typical" or "favorite" *something*. Usually they had already earned their subtitles by the first issue, long before "America" had a chance to read the comic and decide whether or not the character in question was its favorite anything.

*Archie*'s main contender for the girl market during those years was Timely Comics, also called the Marvel Comic Group, under the editorship of Stan Lee. This was the company that would eventually become Marvel Comics, home to superhero comics like *Spiderman* and the *X-Men*, but from 1947 through 1950, they published more teen comics than Archie Publications.

Timely's teen line started in 1944 with *Miss America*. Originally a comic book starring a teenage superheroine of the same name, by its second issue Miss America had become a girls' magazine featuring fiction, fashion and beauty tips, chatty articles about pop stars, and comics. The

**Calling All Girls**, November 1943.

The story of Madame Chiang Kai-shek, from **Calling All Girls**, February 1942.

magazines included advice for teens in comic form, drawn by Phyllis Muchow and a woman who signed her work "Dottie," but *Miss America*'s two main comics featured Miss America herself, a superheroine who fought crime in a cute red skating skirt and harlequin glasses, and a teenage redhead named Patsy Walker. Patsy was to become the company's most popular teenage heroine.

*Miss America* was by no means the first, or the only, girls' magazine to include comics. *Calling All Girls*, started in 1941, was the first, and it did so with such success that within three years its circulation surpassed half a million. *Junior Miss*, published by Timely in 1944, featured comics about teen favorites like Frank Sinatra and June Allyson. But by 1947, the magazine starred comics about a redheaded teenager named Cindy Smith. Cindy got her own book that year, and both that and *Junior Miss* lasted until 1950.

Another girls' magazine, *Keen Teens*, originated in 1945. *Sweet Sixteen* and *Polly Pigtails*, a magazine for the kid sisters of *Calling All Girls* readers, came along in 1946. All of these magazines interspersed comics among their short stories, fashion tips, and gossip about the latest movie stars. *Calling All Girls*, *Sweet Sixteen*, and *Polly Pigtails* were all published by Parents Magazine, and their comics tended to be uplifting tales of real-life role models like Madame Chiang Kai-shek and Louisa May Alcott, or stories about girl reporters. Journalism was one of the few exciting professions open to women in the forties, and comics pages during that decade were filled with girl reporters, from Brenda Starr to Lois Lane.

"Girl Reporter," a "true" comic from **Sweet Sixteen**, May 1947.

Polly Pigtails, March 1947.

A comic about Louisa May Alcott, from **Polly Pigtails**, March 1947.

## MISS PATSY WALKER

None of these girls' magazines lasted beyond 1949, except for *Miss America*, which kept going strong until 1958, in large part thanks to Patsy Walker's spirited stories and snappy dialogue. Patsy was a female variant of Archie; she even had the same red hair. Brunette, rich, and ruthless, Hedy Wolfe was Patsy's Veronica, and they both fought over Buzz Baxter, who worked at Smith's Pharmacy, the Centreville equivalent of Pop's Choklit Shop. But the girls did more than fight over boys. Patsy was as smart as she was pretty. During the early years of her strip, she often quoted poetry, and in at least one story, she proved to be as much of a feminist as Little Lulu. In a 1945 story drawn by Ruth Atkinson, Patsy discovers that girls are paid twelve dollars a week for after-school jobs, while boys earn eighteen dollars for the same work. "Why should boys get more money than girls," she asks, "—that's unfair!" She organizes a protest with her girlfriends, announcing, "We'll organize a world movement for equal rights for women…" and "We're going to liberate all womankind!" The girls protest by wearing slacks instead of skirts to school, by carrying their own books, and by paying their way at movies and the soda shop. Unfortunately for them, Hedy Wolfe, the lone holdout, refuses to wear slacks and goes over to the "boys'" side. The boys put up a big sign headlined "Woman Power Shortage," and they all sign up for dates with Hedy.

In an ending that's a bit of a letdown, a now dateless Patsy complains to the other girls, "Are equal rights worth the loss of one's boyfriend?…A thousand times no! Let's get busy, women!" She convinces the school principal to

Patsy demands equality, from **Patsy Walker** no.2, 1945. Drawn by Ruth Atkinson.

Girls' Life, no.1, January 1954. Cover by Al Hartley.

Patsy's friend Nancy, drawn by Pauline Loth, quoting poetry, from **Miss America**, April 1946.

institute a dress code forbidding slacks at school, and the girls, now in skirts, win back their boyfriends. By the end of the story, the original problem of unequal pay has been forgotten in favor of the importance of boyfriends. Nevertheless, the subject matter is pretty revolutionary for a comic written twenty-five years before the women's liberation movement.

Patsy Walker was rewarded with her own book by 1945, and during her twenty-two-year run starred in a half dozen titles, including *Patsy and Hedy*, *A Date with Patsy*, *Patsy and Her Pals*, and *Patsy Walker's Fashion Parade*. Even her rival, Hedy Wolfe, got her own comic book in 1957. Patsy was such a success that in 1953 her publishers came up with a Patsy clone named Wendy Parker. Wendy was drawn by Christopher Rule, who had also drawn Patsy, so the two heroines looked alike, but she was a college student instead of a high school girl. This gave Rule the excuse to dress his heroine in high heels and sophisticated party dresses, the likes of which no college student ever wore. Despite the book's beautiful art, Wendy was no Patsy Walker, and she only lasted eight issues.

By far the most unusual *Patsy Walker* spin-off was *Girls' Life*, subtitled "Patsy Walker's Own Magazine for Girls!" This combination comic book and magazine, which lasted for six issues in 1954, was supposedly edited by Patsy Walker herself! On the title page, Patsy Walker is credited as editor, and Stan Lee is called "editorial and art director." Although its format was straight comic book, the contents of *Girls' Life* were all magazine. There was only one *Patsy Walker* comic inside, and the rest of the book contained short stories, fashion articles, diet tips, a beauty section (Patsy's comment on bras: "*Please* remember in choosing a bra that it is intended only as support, not a bandage!"), two pages on parties called "Partying with Patsy," and an advice column

**("Dear Patsy, I am fourteen years old. Some of the girls in my class wear lipstick, but my mother says I am too young to use it. What do you think?"**

Patsy's advice: "Forget about lipstick until your mother says you're finally old enough to wear it."). Everything was ostensibly written by the red-haired teenager, which may make *Girls' Life* the only magazine ever edited by a fictional comic character.

Nellie the Nurse, April 1948.

Along with *Miss America* magazine, the year 1944 also saw the debut of *Tessie the Typist*, the first of Timely's "career girl" comic books. Actually, like Suzie, Tessie is already out of school, but she's a whole lot smarter than the *Archie* heroine; in fact, she's not even a typist in that first issue. Instead, she holds down three jobs, all reflecting in one way or another the war being fought overseas. In the first story, Tessie is hired as a lion tamer by a circus whose animal trainers are all in the service. In the second, she's a showgirl entertaining the troops, and in the last, she gets a job in a factory where the foreman, mistaking her for a dumb blond, puts her in charge of a broken machine. Not only is the machine broken, but nobody has a clue about what the machine did when it worked. Tessie fixes the machine, and it starts spitting out tanks by the hundreds. The delighted foreman exclaims, "It was a stroke of genius! Only a master mechanic who knew physics and electronics could have done it! *How* did you do it?" Tessie holds up a hairpin: "I-I just stuck this little hairpin in here when no one was looking…"

By 1945, two more Timely career girl comics were keeping *Tessie* company on the newsstands: *Nellie the Nurse* and *Millie the Model*. Editor and writer Stan Lee, who seemed to have a flair for alliteration, later came up with yet another career girl: *Sherry the Showgirl*. Obviously, girls found the modeling profession more glamorous than that of nursing, for while Nellie had a respectable run, surviving until 1957, *Millie* really took off. She soon acquired a respectable number of spin-off titles, including *Life with Millie, Mad About Millie, Modeling with Millie*, and *A Date with Millie*, and lasted longer than any of Timely's girl titles, staying in print for twenty-eight years.

The stories in *Millie the Model* were gen-

Tessie's wartime message, from **Tessie the Typist** no.1, 1944.

erally lightweight, revolving around the rivalry of Millie and her red-haired nemesis, Chili Seven, over modeling jobs and over Millie's longtime boyfriend, a photographer named Clicker. But in a 1955 issue, Millie was forced to confront the then-accepted tradition of women leaving their careers for marriage.

The story, drawn by Dan DeCarlo, opens with Millie and Clicker on a park bench. Clicker finally proposes: "Millie, we've been going together for years now… and it's about time we talked about marriage!" At first Millie is thrilled ("I've got the church all picked out…and the minister…and my gown…"), but Clicker interrupts her, "Hold on, honey…there's *one* thing…if we get married, you've *got* to give up modeling!" He explains further, "Because I want you to stay home and take care of our house!" This was unbeatable logic in 1955, and Millie accepts it.

**Millie the Model**, October 1947. Art by Ken Bald.

# HEDY DE VINE

COMING SOON STARRING FEARLESS HEDY DE VINE in JUNGLE QUEEN

"NO MORE LEGS!"

SQUEAK! SQUEAK!

"O.K.! I'll give it up, if it'll make **YOU** happy!" But as the story progresses, and Millie gives notice at the modeling agency, she starts looking more and more miserable. She and Clicker sit in a restaurant together, and he's happy as a clam. "I was **PROUD** of you, honey!" he says. "You quit just for **ME**!" The corners of Millie's mouth are turned way down, and all she can muster is, "Uh-huh . . ." Walking home, Clicker continues cluelessly, "Aren't you happy you gave up modeling? After all, I didn't want you to work any more and the man is boss, right?" Finally, he can no longer ignore the tears pouring down Millie's cheeks. "Millie," he asks innocently, "Is something wrong?" By the last panel, Clicker has relented, a happy Millie has gone back to work, and everything is as it was before. Clicker and Millie never did marry, but remained engaged for the book's twenty-eight-year run, a record for long engagements.

In 1947, another Timely Comics career girl, Hedy DeVine, entered the picture. Hedy was a blond movie star, and her name was obviously based on 1940s actress Hedy Lamarr. (Lest Lana Turner be jealous, Timely came up with a showgirl named Lana a year later.) A later addition to Timely's career girl line was *Meet Miss Bliss*, prettily drawn in 1955 by Al Hartley. Miss Bliss couldn't have been more different from Timely's showgirls, models, and movie stars—she was an attractive schoolteacher, admired by her students and wooed by at least two handsome colleagues. Alas, a wholesome and intelligent schoolteacher was just not glamorous enough for young girl readers, and the title only ran for four issues.

Hedy DeVine, from **Millie the Model**, June 1948. Art by Ed Winiarski.

One of the most unusual of Timely's career girl series was *Annie Oakley*, which hit the stands in 1948. Rather than re-creating the escapades of the famous nineteenth-century sharpshooter, the story took place in the contemporary American West. In the first story, Bruce Barr, owner of the Barr-X Ranch, is talking with his pretty brunette secretary, Sally: "We just have to find a new **RANCH-HAND**! We're terribly short of help this season!" The door opens and in walks a "6 foot hunk of man…Tex Collins, foreman…" "I found the extra hand you were looking for!" he announces. Sally starts preening: "Who is he, Tex? Is he good-looking? Have I ever seen him before?" Tex grins. "You'd be surprised, Sally!" and orders, "Slim, have that new cowpuncher brought in!" Slim exclaims, "Boy, I ain't never seed such a hand! What a shot! What a roper! What a rider!" Finally we see the new ranch hand—a beautiful blond dressed in a short fringed buckskin dress, astride a prancing horse. *"He's a her!"* says Tex.

Annie Oakley in action, from **Annie Oakley** no.1, 1948.

Sally feels jealous and threatened. "How can a girl take a job meant for a man?" she objects. "Silliest thing I ever heard! Why, you can't have a girl roping cattle, riding and branding! Girls can't do that kind of work!" But of course Annie proves to be a real hero. She saves Sally from a raging bull, and goes on to become world champion at the rodeo. Annie Oakley's message seems to be that a girl can be as good, if not better, than a guy, and still get boyfriends.

But the company was not neglecting their teenagers, and by 1948, *Margie*, *Mitzi*, *Rusty*, and *Jeanie* occupied magazine racks next to *Patsy Walker* and *Cindy*, while teenage boys were represented by *Oscar*, *Willie*, *Georgie*, and *Frankie*. Even Timely's boy comics sometimes tackled girls' issues like the omnipresent boys' club—but from a boy's point of view. In a *Georgie* comic from 1948, the boys form a new club, "The Laurelton Young Men's Athletic Club." Georgie calls the meeting to order and announces, "We don't want **GIRLS** in our club! Girls always start trouble—our club will be for **MEN ONLY**!" But Georgie's girlfriend, Judy, passes by the clubhouse, sees a meeting going on, and comes in. At first, Georgie asks her to leave: "This meeting is for **BOYS ONLY**!"—but the other boys plead her case. "Let her stay!"

Georgie and the boys' club, from **Patsy Walker** no.15, 1948. Art by Mike Sekowski.

Cindy has dog trouble, from **Cindy** no.27, 1947.
Art by Ken Bald.

they urge, adding, "Don't be a **SORE-HEAD**!" Unfortunately, once she's allowed in the club, Judy wants to redecorate: "What you really need are nice pink curtains and drapes!" In the last panel, Judy sits in front of the clubhouse, presumably where she landed when she was tossed out. A voice from within the clubhouse shouts, "And **STAY** out!" while Judy exclaims, "**MEN! BAH!**"

Most of the Marvel Comic Group's teen and career girl comics were written by Stan Lee, and they tended to follow the formula of the eternal triangle: a girl, a boy, and a rival. Just as there was, and still is, a recognizable *Archie* style, there was, by 1947, a definite Timely Comics style—crisp, lively, and accessible. The boys might sometimes look funny, but all the girls were pretty. They dressed in rolled-up jeans and sweaters or cute dresses, and spent their time at the soda shop. Like a good many of the other comic companies' teen comics, Timely's books often featured reader-designed paper dolls depicting their heroines.

The artist for the first *Miss America* and *Patsy Walker* stories was Pauline Loth, a one-time animation artist who doubled as the magazine's fashion editor. Later, *Patsy Walker* stories in the magazine were drawn by Christopher Rule, the most elegant of the Patsy Walker artists, who also illustrated short stories and fashion features. Rule was somewhat older than most of the other artists who drew Patsy, and his rendition of her is polished and stylish. While during the war years women like Pauline Loth and Ruth Atkinson did much of the art— Atkinson drew the first issue of *Millie the Model* and most of the first two years' worth of *Patsy Walker*—after the war, as in every other industry, the men came back from overseas and took back the work. Some of them, despite working in the house style, had a distinctive look to their art. Ken Bald, who drew both Millie and Cindy, produced pages that were almost art deco, incorporating bold checkerboard designs and panels in which he turned sound effects into decoration with the aid of bold primary colors.

Since the color used in printing comics of that period was anything but subtle, there were really only three colors to choose from for hair— yellow, red, and black. Thus, redheaded Cindy and Nellie had black-haired Sandra and Pam

**Candy**, January 1956.

for rivals, blond Hedy DeVine's rival was a red-haired actress named Sandra Stiles, and blond Millie's nemesis was the spectacular red-haired model Chili Seven, the only professional rival besides Veronica who was so much fun that for four years she starred in her own comic book.

In a 1948 list of forty-nine monthly comics published by Timely Comics, twenty-seven were aimed at girls. Not so coincidentally, as many or sometimes more girls than boys were reading comics. The cover of *Patsy Walker* no. 17 boasted "Over 5 million readers!" and a 1953 ad claimed 6 million. Clearly, Timely Comics and Archie Publications were at the top of the teen comics market, but other companies were quick to recognize a good thing.

One of the first, and most charming, comics to climb onto the teen bandwagon was *Taffy*, which was better than its life span, 1945 to 1948, might indicate. Unlike many of the other curvy comic-book teen queens, Taffy and her toothy friend Putty were drawn by artist Mort Leav as skinny thirteen-year-olds. The girls were no glamourpusses, but they were adorable. Like many of the other teen titles, *Taffy* included stories about real movie stars, pop singers, and other teen faves. A 1947 issue features "America's No. 1 covergirl," Candy Jones, showing Taffy how to become a model or look just like one. Among her tips:"Treat yourself to a well fitted girdle."

*Candy*, first published in 1947 by Quality Comics and subtitled "America's Favorite Teenage Girl," was another toothy teenager whose perky escapades earned her a nine-year run on the newsstands. On the other hand, *Sunny*, published that same year by Fox Comics and subtitled "America's Sweetheart," was the school tramp. Fox was rightly

**Taffy**, November 1946. Cover by L. B. Cole.

A 1947 ad for the Marvel Comic Group's teen comics.

known as a comic company that specialized in lurid and slightly trashy comics. Artist Al Feldstein put his teen heroine in tight, low-cut dresses that showed off her exaggerated cleavage and pointy breasts. While Patsy Walker quoted poetry and Candy wore cute ballet shoes, Sunny flunked biology and wore spike heels to school. Feldstein even put the poor kid into high-heeled ice skates! Mercifully, she lasted only a year.

As early as 1946, a graph in *Newsdealer* magazine had shown that in the age groups eight to eleven years, and again at eighteen to thirty-four years, female comic-book readers outnumbered males. By the late 1940s, teen comics aimed at girls outnumbered crime comics, horror comics, and superhero comics. The sky was the limit.

Sorority Sue, one of the only college girls in comics, from **Dotty**, June 1948. Art by Vince Fago.

Teen titles kept coming from more than a dozen publishers through the forties and early fifties: *Algie, Kathy, Cindy, Linda, Vicky, Mazie, My Girl Pearl, Miss Beverly Hills of Hollywood, Della Vision, Slick Chicks,* and *Popular Teenagers*. Comic-book readers in 1948 could read about the adventures of Dotty, a hatcheck girl at the El Kisco club, and Sorority Sue, the only other college girl in teen comics besides Wendy Parker. Dotty was nicely drawn by Al Hartley, who later drew *Patsy Walker*; Vince Fago, who had been the editor of *Miss America* when it started in 1944, drew *Sorority Sue*. At about the same time, teenage girl newspaper strips like Hilda Terry's "Teena" and Linda and Jerry Walters' "Susie Q. Smith" were being reprinted in comic-book form. There was even a science-fiction teen comic called *Jetta*, subtitled "Teen-Age Sweetheart of the 21st

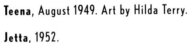

**Teena**, August 1949. Art by Hilda Terry.

**Jetta**, 1952.

**Sunny**, with pointy bra and high-heeled ice skates, 1947. Art by Al Feldstein.

**Susie Q. Smith**, 1951. Art by Linda Walters.

Century," which predated *The Jetsons* by a good ten years. The futuristic teenagers in *Jetta* used expressions like "Well, split my atoms!" Girls were "space pigeons," and instead of Pop's Choklit Shop, the gang buzzed over to "Joe's Blast-Inn for a chocolate fission fizz."

Meanwhile, there were plenty more *Archie* wanna-bes. DC Comics never quite got into publishing teen comics with the zeal exhibited by Timely, and most of the few they produced, for whatever odd reasoning on the part of their editorial staff, starred boys rather than girls. *Buzzy* ("America's Favorite Teen-ager!") was published by them from 1944 through 1958. From Prize Publications came *Dudley* ("The Teen-age Sensation!"), a truly wacko comic by Boodie Rogers that started in 1947 and featured a teenage hero who

Archie wanna-bes. Top to bottom: Buzzy, Dudley, Merton.

"Melody," from **Meet Merton**, 1954. Art by Gill Fox.

was hooked on food and expressed himself with phrases like "Hot yam from Alabam!", "Gee from Kankakee!", and

# "Butter my ears and call me Toasty!"

Dudley lasted a year, as did *Meet Merton*, a comparative latecomer drawn from 1953 to 1954 by Dave Berg.

A backup story in *Meet Merton* was "Melody," beautifully drawn by Gill Fox. Melody's last name was—wouldn't you know it?—Lane, and she was as resourceful as she was cute. Somehow, even if Melody's plans didn't always work out as expected, they still worked out. In a 1954 story, Melody buys barbells as a birthday present for her boyfriend, Rupert, and perfume for her mother. When the barbells are delivered to her mother, she realizes the packages have been mixed up and races back to the store, hoping to retrieve the perfume before it's delivered to Rupert. She snatches the still undelivered perfume, but a clerk mistakes her for a thief and Melody, now a fugitive hiding out in the sportswear department from the police, climbs into a diving suit. Along comes Rupert's rich aunt Abigail, who buys the diving suit for her nephew and has it delivered to his birthday party. Rupert unwraps his present, and out steps Melody. Her boyfriend exclaims, "What an original and clever way to come to a party!" Melody's artist, Gill Fox, had been one of the artists on the "dumb blond" strip "Torchy," but Melody was a whole lot smarter (and she dressed better).

In 1950, the Marvel Comic Group started publishing their own "dumb blond" comic, *My Friend Irma*. Irma was written by Stan Lee and drawn by Dan DeCarlo, who had taken over the art on *Millie the Model* the previous year and would go on to become, next to Bob Montana, the definitive Betty and Veronica artist. Irma said **"Golly!"** a lot, and survived for five years on the simple premise of her dim bulb. Some examples: Irma, buying a black puppy, to the clerk at a pet store: "What's his name?" Clerk: "Blackie!" Irma: **"Golly!** With a name like that, it's lucky he's black!" Irma's room-mate, Jane: "Irma…you ought to find a hobby!" Irma: "Why… did anybody **LOSE** one?" Jane: "Like painting, for instance! Have you ever dabbled in oil?" Irma: **"Golly, no!** I use soap and water!" It was a one-joke comic, and despite Dan DeCarlo's lively art, it got pretty tired after a while.

*My Friend Irma* was based on successful radio and television shows, which in turn were based on a movie, all of them starring actress Marie Wilson, so Stan Lee can't be blamed for inventing the character. Archie, the first and longest-lasting comic teenager, had been on the radio since 1945, and other comic publishers adapted teen films and radio shows quicker than you could say, "Don't touch that dial." DC Comics came up with *A Date with Judy*, based on the radio show and film, in 1947, and in 1960 published a comic version of the television hit *The Many Loves of Dobie Gillis*. Dell Comics published *Henry Aldrich* and *Andy Hardy*, both during the first half of the fifties. Charlton Comics published their comic-book version of the hit television show *My Little Margie* in 1954, complete with the then ubiquitous reader-designed paper dolls. The comic lasted ten years and even had a companion title, *My Little Margie's Boyfriends*, for three of those years.

Another radio show, *Meet Corliss Archer*, was turned into a comic in 1948 by Fox, the same publishers who had produced trashy little *Sunny*, and Corliss was drawn in the same style by the same artist. In fact, when Dr. Frederick Wertham wrote his influential 1954 book *Seduction of the Innocents*, in which he claimed comics led to juvenile delinquency, he reprinted panels from all three issues of the comic as damning evidence of girls' distorted sexual image in comics. The result is that issues of *Meet Corliss Archer* are avidly sought after by comics collectors (mostly men), who are willing to pay more than one hundred dollars for a first addition, simply because the girl on the cover has big breasts.

Ad for **My Friend Irma**, from **Millie the Model** no.23, 1950. Art by Dan DeCarlo.

**My Little Margie** paper dolls, October 1960. Art by Jon D'Agostino.

**A Date with Judy**, November 1957.

The majority of these teen titles had a short life span, lasting at most no more than a few years. The teen comic mania was already winding down by the end of the forties, and the greater part of Timely's many teen titles had gone to that heavenly newsstand in the sky by 1949. *Willie* and *Cindy* clung to life for another year, and *Hedy DeVine* and *Georgie* made it until 1952.

The **Archie** comics line, still going strong in 1955.

The mid- to late-fifties was not a good time for any comics, teen or otherwise. Sales of all comics had been steadily declining during the decade, due partly to the burgeoning popularity of television and partly to Wertham's book, which caused many parents to stop buying comics for their kids. Wertham based his conclusions on interviews with children in reform school that showed all of them were comics readers. Using the same logic, we could prove that tomatoes turn people into killers by showing that 99 percent of the residents of our prisons' death rows regularly eat tomatoes.

At the end of the fifties, only the unbeatable Archie comics were still going strong. While other teen comics were dropping like flies, Archie actually initiated new titles. *Archie's Girls, Betty and Veronica, Archie's Mad House, Archie's Mechanics, Archie's Pals 'n' Gals, Little Archie,* and *Archie's Rival, Reggie* all came out during the 1950s.

By 1957, *Nellie the Nurse* had emptied her last bedpan, and the Marvel Comic Group had canceled most of their superhero and adventure titles. *Patsy Walker* and *Millie the Model* were all that was left of their once great line of teen comics. But by then, girls had found something else to interest them: romance comics.

# Chapter Two

# Women's Comics

## 1947–1977

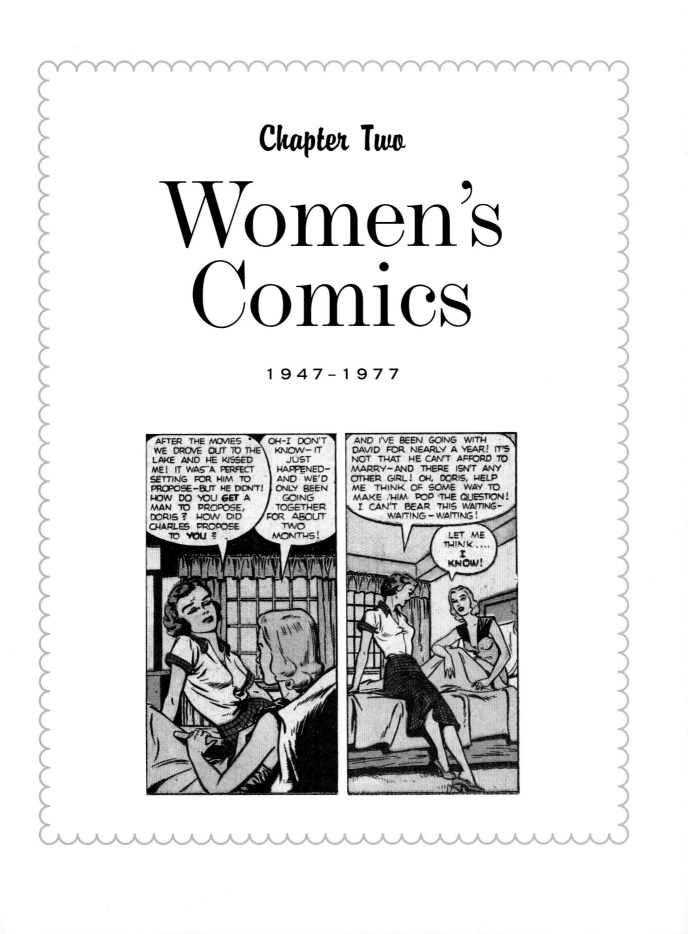

**LOVE** was nothing new to the world of comics. After all, that's what prompted Betty and Veronica to fight over Archie, and Patsy Walker and Hedy Wolfe to battle over Buzz Baxter. Even Clark Kent had to compete with his own alter ego, Superman, for the affections of Lois Lane. But that kind of love consisted of dancing together at the prom and sharing sodas at the Choklit Shop. Nobody ever kissed, and nobody ever cried—until 1947. That was the year that two ex-GIs named Joe Simon and Jack Kirby created a comic book called *My Date*.

The Simon and Kirby team was already established in comics by 1947. Before the war, they had created well-known superhero comics like *Captain America* and boys' adventures like *The Boy Commandos* and *The Newsboy Legion*. But *My Date* was unique—a comic that definitely appealed to female readers. Most of the book consisted of variations on the teen comics so popular at the time: the misadventures of a freckled blond bobby-soxer named Ginny, or of Swifty Chase and his girlfriend, Sunny Daye. But each issue also included a love story told in first person. These were modeled after the stories in magazines like *Personal Romances*, *True Experiences*, and *True Confessions*, avidly read by women since the first romance magazine, *True Story*, started in 1920. Supposedly, "I Was a Tomboy Too Long," "Mine Were Coward's Kisses," "Whisper My Name," and "Because His Lips Thrilled" were true stories, told by the women who had experienced them. Whether the women reading these stories believed they were true is something we may never know, but judging from their enormous success, it didn't matter.

The idea of a love story in comic form obviously struck a chord with slightly older readers, who wanted more than lighthearted teenage humor. *My Date* only lasted four issues, but before it ended its run, Simon and Kirby had produced America's first romance comic book, aptly titled *Young Romance*. While the age of teen comics readers had ranged from ten to teen, *Young Romance*'s cover bore a banner declaring, "Designed for the more adult readers of comics." In this case, *adult* meant girls in the early to late teens, although judging from the letter columns, a good number of readers were also young housewives, the same women who devoured romance magazines.

In his 1990 autobiographical book, *The Comic Book Makers*, co-written with his son Jim, Joe Simon remembers he and Jack Kirby seeing "a group of at least a dozen teenage girls in bobby sox…gathered around the newsstand rifling through the pages of the newly arrived *Young Romance Comics* (Number 1), giggling and squealing with delight.

" 'I hope they put out more of these,' one of the girls exclaimed. The others agreed in shrill sounds.

"Jack and I were as excited as the girls."

The banner may have said "adult," but stories with torrid titles like "I Was a Pickup," "Back Door Love," and "You're Not the First" promised more than they delivered. In "Back Door Love," the heroine secretly dates a man her

A couple of world-weary Simon and Kirby women in an ad for **Young Romance**, 1948.

**Young Romance**, January-February 1948. Art by Joe Simon and Jack Kirby.

parents disapprove of. The protagonist of "You're Not the First" simply went out with a lot of guys before marrying, and her husband gets jealous. There was no mention of sex; girls got bad reputations from *kissing* too many men. Nevertheless, the cast of characters in the Simon and Kirby comics were down and dirty—literally. The working-class hero might be an auto mechanic, and the heroine a waitress. The most a woman in these early love comics could aspire to was the position of nurse or private secretary, and they always gave it all up anyway to get married and become housewives.

Occasionally the Simon and Kirby team handled grown-up themes, thinly disguised. In a 1949 story titled "Different" ("The story they dared us to

"The Haunting Past," from **Miss America**, circa 1949-50. Art by Valerie Barclay.

print!"), Irma, the heroine, has a father who comes from Europe, and has changed his name from Jacoby Wilheim to Jack Williams. When their small-town neighbors discover his origins, they shun him. Irma and her family are called "foreigners" and "your kind," but the word *Jew* is never used, although the story is obviously about anti-Semitism. Jack Kirby must have had a personal stake in this story, because his own real name was Jacob Kurtzberg.

Both Kirby and Simon shared in the writing and the art, and their comics had a look that distinguished them from the multitude of love comics that followed. Their panels had a dark, film noir look to them, their men were high-cheekboned and earthy, often appearing, Stanley Kowalski style, in undershirts, and their women had shiny, dark, Joan Crawford lips and world-weary expressions. They had been around the block a few times.

The first issue of *Young Romance* sold 92 percent of its print run, and by its third issue the print run tripled. Within two years the comic was joined on the newsstands by *Young Love*, then *Young Brides* (1952) and *In Love* (1954). Simon and Kirby were selling well over one million copies of their romance titles every month.

"Date Snatcher," from **My Date**, November 1947.

Other publishers knew a trend when they saw it, and many added love comics to their already existing teen comics line. Within a year, Timely, a major publisher of teen comics, had produced its first love comic, *My Romance*, and at the same time, Fox ceased publication of their teen book, *Meet Corliss Archer*, and switched to *My Life*. Even the teen magazine *Miss America* added love comics to its pages, and Timely's superheroine title, *Venus*, became

Waitresses in love, from **Sweethearts**, April 1949.

a love comic. In one year—1948 to 1949—romance comic titles jumped from four to 125. By 1950, more than one quarter of the comic books published were romance comics. This was the same year that a graph in *Newsdealer* magazine showed that females age seventeen to twenty-five were reading more comic books than guys. It doesn't take a rocket scientist to figure out what kind of comics they were reading.

Further proof of the romance comics' 99 percent female readership were the ads for dresses that ran in many issues ("Sheer enchantment of exotic nylon tulle preludes a passionate contrasting bodice and flower studded underskirt. Sheer stole adds touch of deviltry to your bare shoulders."), and the letters, too perfect to have been made up:

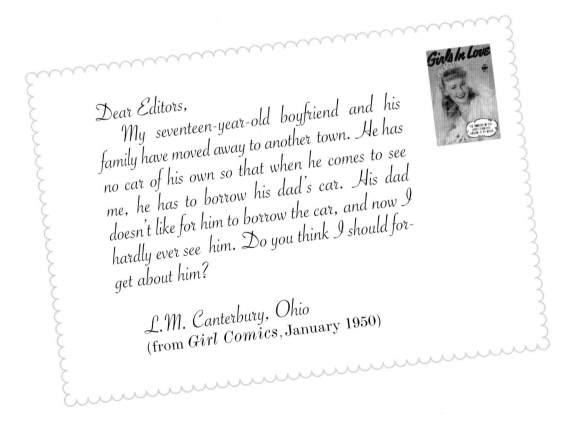

Dear Editors,
My seventeen-year-old boyfriend and his family have moved away to another town. He has no car of his own so that when he comes to see me, he has to borrow his dad's car. His dad doesn't like for him to borrow the car, and now I hardly ever see him. Do you think I should forget about him?

L. M. Canterbury, Ohio
(from *Girl Comics*, January 1950)

Florida Fashions for only $2.98! An ad from **Girl Comics**, January 1950.

Hi-School Romance, October 1953.

Although they shared certain traditions—the villain always had a pencil-thin mustache!—love comics were not as generic as people today believe. Some love comics had special themes. The heroines of *Cinderella Love* always met their Prince Charming, and the women of *Career Girl Romances* all had good jobs, even though love usually proved more important than career. *Wartime Romances*, published during the Korean War, is self-explanatory. As for the themes of

# Hi-School Romance, High School Confidential Diary, Teen-Age Romance, Teen-Age Temptations, Teen Confessions, and Teen Secret Diary,

you get three guesses.

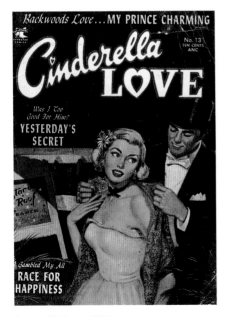

Cinderella Love, 1953.

Career Girl Romances, February 1968.
Art by R. Garcia.

Wartime Romances, March 1952.
Art by Matt Baker.

Ad for a whole passel of western romance comics, all published by the Marvel Comic Group circa 1949-50.

Some of the more enterprising publishers even decided to combine the then popular western comics with their romance comics, and came up with titles such as *Rangeland Love, Cowboy Love, Golden West Love, Frontier Romances, Cowboy Romances, Cowgirl Romances, Range Romances, Saddle Romances, Western Life Romances, Real West Romances, Flaming Western Romances, Romances of the West, Romantic Western, Western Hearts,* and *Western Love Trails.* (But there was no *Geriatric Romance* or *Mid-Life Crisis Confessions.* In the romance comics world of the late forties and fifties, over thirty meant over the hill.)

Sometimes the personality of a particular romance title reflected the publisher's or editor's personal tastes. In love comics published by Fawcett Publications during the late 1940s and early 1950s, the woman was always at fault, and needed a man to lead her from the error of her ways. Out of three stories in every issue, at least one—often more—ended sadly because of some terrible mistake the woman had made. In the last panel, with the requisite tear rolling down her cheek, the heroine sobs out a variation on this rather confusing sentence from *Romantic Secrets,* September 1952: "…sob…if somehow, others could learn by this heartbreak that is mine . . . without waiting to discover their wrongs, too late!" We will never know if the editor was simply a misogynist or if, like the characters in his comics, he had suffered terribly in some love affair gone wrong.

Timely's love comics were among the most interesting—they tended to combine romance with adventure or drama. In "House of Shadows" (subtitled "Thrilling Because It's True!"), from *Girl Comics* no. 7, Marge's new husband, Chet, buys a rundown little house in Greenwich, Connecticut, believing it's the honeymoon cottage of her dreams.

The National romance group, mid-fifties. National is now DC Comics.

The girl's to blame! "I Won't Forget," from **Romantic Secrets**, September 1952. Art by Bob Powell.

He doesn't know that his wife was once married to Rocky, a convicted thief who stashed $100,000 somewhere in the house before he was caught and sent to prison, and that every day when he's off at work, she searches the house for the loot. But Marge is already having second thoughts. "Poor Chet!" she thinks. "One of these days I'll find what I've been looking for, and he'll come home from work to find me gone…his little dream world shattered to dust! Oh, why did it have to be a decent guy like that?" Just as Marge finally finds the money, Rocky, who has escaped from prison, arrives to hold them both at gunpoint. Chet realizes the truth: "Marge, Marge! You never cared for me…you just played me for a sap…" But when Rocky shoots at Chet, Marge throws herself in front of the bullet, saving his life. In the last scene, Marge recovers from the gunshot wound in the hospital, while Chet hovers over her bed. "Oh Chet…my darling Chet!" she tells him, "I'll spend the rest of my days proving how much you mean to me!"

Another dramatic story in the same issue, "Black-Out!", was obviously inspired by the Alfred Hitchcock film *Suspicion*. Paula's convinced that her husband, Jim, is planning to murder her. "He wants to get rid of me…because I'm no longer young enough for him!" As the story progresses, she becomes more and more neurotic. In a scene right out of the movie, Jim offers her a glass of milk at bedtime to calm her. She knocks it out of his hand: "That's poison! You want to kill me…you murderer!" The story ends at a cliff's edge. Joan Fontaine—oops, Paula—pursued through a storm by her husband, attempts to throw herself off the cliff ("Death would free me from the fear that gripped me!"), only to be grabbed in midair by Jim. "Let me go!" she screams. "Let me die the way I want to die!" But of course, Paula's only having a nervous breakdown, and in the last panel she's been cured, and is reunited with her husband, while her shrink tells a smiling nurse, "She's completely recovered from her breakdown!"

By issue no. 6, *Girl Comics* had morphed into a unique adventure series in which the heroines' adventures were stressed over the romance angle. Often, there was no romance at all, and instead of a boyfriend the heroine interacted with her brother or father. In "The Horns," from issue 6, Lalita is a bullfighter whose father, Manuelo, was "…once the most famous of all toreadors, once respected and adored…until that disgraceful day" when he "turned coward in the arena…fled the ring in fear of the bull…and…disappeared." What no one knows is that Manuelo suddenly became blind in the arena. Now he warns his daughter, "Blindness in our family is hereditary! It may strike you at any moment…as it did me…in the ring…**AS YOU FACE THE HORNS OF THE BULL!**" Bravely, his daughter answers, "The horns hold no terror for me, my father! Even blind I will not shrink from them!" But the next day, facing the bull in the arena, she thinks, "…My eyes are growing dim!…Merciful heavens! I can't see! I am blind!" Lalita turns to run from the bull as the crowd, unaware of her sudden blindness, shouts, "**COWARD! COWARD!**", "**LIKE FATHER, LIKE DAUGHTER!**" and "**TWO OF A KIND!**" She stops and faces the bull: "For the honor of my father I shall face the horns!" "At the last second," says the caption, "the blade flashed in the brilliance of the Spanish sun! Lalita had killed her last bull!" As the crowd shouts, "**VIVA LALITA!**" and "**VIVA MANUELO!**", the blind father and daughter stumble off, hand in hand.

Some of the comics got pretty sordid—or as sordid as they were allowed to get in those days. Since divorce was considered shocking, and premarital sex didn't even exist in the comic-book world, the only way to show that one of the main characters was not a virgin was to stick her or him with a previous marriage. In the 1952 story "Her Man or Mine?" from *All True Romance*, the heroine's fiancé is a soldier whose hasty wartime marriage had been annulled. Then his first wife, a true floozy in ankle-strap shoes, shows up, claiming they're still

"How Did He Propose?," from **Lovers' Lane**, February 1950. Art by Ruth Atkinson.

"I Was a Love Gypsy," a stylish page from **Teen-Age Romance**, February 1952. Art by Matt Baker.

married and demanding blackmail money. The hero arrives in the nick of time with proof of the annulment, but not before a good catfight between the floozy and the bride-to-be.

An even seamier story was "No Greater Love," from the February 1953 issue of *True Love*. In a plot right out of a Barbara Stanwyk movie, Mary, working as a waitress to support her shiftless, unemployed husband, is three months pregnant when he asks for a divorce so he can marry a rich widow. (But the word *pregnant*, considered almost obscene in the fifties, was never used in a comic. Instead she says, "I'm going to be a mother in six months.") "I saw my life shattered before my eyes by the weakling I had once called my husband," runs the caption. Mary throws the bum out, grants him a divorce, and gives the baby up for adoption. A year later ("a year of yearning for my baby"), she sneaks a peek into the adoption agency's files, and finds the address of her baby's new parents. Without revealing her identity, Mary befriends little Jimmy's adoptive parents, and dates his handsome uncle. Of course the worthless ex-husband, dumped by the widow, comes back. Mary finds out he's blackmailing their baby's new parents ("You're even lower than I thought...using your own child as a pawn!"), and goes to them with the truth, but it turns out that they knew all along, and have been tape recording his shakedowns. Faced with "charges of defamation, extortion, blackmail, and a few others," the no-good ex-husband leaves town, and the handsome uncle proposes to Mary. "Y-you mean you still want me?" she wonders. "After—" In the last-panel clinch, he replies, "We can't let Jimmy grow up with no playmates."

This alludes to an interestingly tangled future in which little Jimmy's aunt is also his mother, and his cousins are his siblings. If his adoptive parents then give birth to a biological child who marries one of his natural mother's children, would he become his own brother-in-law?

No matter how the various love comics differed, they all had one thing in common: in the end, true happiness came to every woman only with the love of the right man, and the traditional role of wife and homemaker. Prissie Welldon, the heroine of "No Escape!" from *Girl Comics* no. 1, October 1949, wants "adventure, excitement, thrills! I dreamt of competing with men on their own grounds!" But her father tells her, "Never mind, Prissie! You'll be starting on an adventure of your own some day—when you get married!"

# "Oh, why did I have to be born a girl?!!"

cries Prissie, who then convinces her father to give her enough money to open a restaurant in Alaska. She opens her restaurant in the town of Tough Luck, Alaska, and meets the local hunk, Mark Dobson, but other things are more important than romance: "I had to stick to my plan, I told myself—a real career with no feminine side-trackings."

But Prissie finds it impossible to keep order among the rough-and-tumble men who frequent her restaurant, and one night, cleaning up after a pie-throwing brawl, she vows, "Nobody pays attention to a girl in a lace apron! From now on I'm going to be just as tough as they are!", and she dons blue jeans. Her customers don't seem to mind: "As long as you don't lose that feminine touch with the vittles, Prissie!"

Then one night, Big Ben Hogan, the local bad guy, enters with his

*Produced by* SIMON & KIRBY

There's always one kid in a crowd to spoil things for the others-- the kid who gives the rest of the gang a bad name!--In our crowd his name was Peter Nelson, a wild, reckless ne'er do well who was in love with speed!--WHO LOVED THE TON OF METAL HE CALLED A HOT ROD, ALMOST AS MUCH AS I LOVED HIM!-- And I was forced to become a part of this race to destruction!

**Would our love last through the mad pace set by the thrill-crazed HOT ROD CROWD!**

cronies, intending to rob her. With only Mark Dobson there fighting the whole gang off, Prissie ducks into the back room, changes out of her jeans, and emerges, wearing "the fanciest dress I owned…" Fluffing up her hairdo, she says, "…you don't really want to hold me up, do you? How about settling for some ham 'n' eggs?"

And it works! "Rob Miss Welldon?" exclaims one hood, "Over my dead body!" Another adds, "We was just… uh…feeling our oats a little too much tonight, I reckon!" Finally we see Prissie and Mark in the required clinch. He says, "See what I mean, Prissie? There's nothing more powerful in the world than a pretty girl!", to which she answers, "I guess from now on, I'll forget my silly notion of trying to act like a man!"

During the fifties, classic films such as *Rebel Without a Cause*, *The Blackboard Jungle*, and *The Wild Ones*, as well as the more trashy *Problem Girls*, *Hot Rod Girl*, and *So Young, So Bad*, all exemplified the American public's interest and concern with juvenile delinquency. Romance comics were quick to exploit the countrywide fascination with teen gangs, and none did so as well as the original love comics creators, Simon and Kirby, with stories like "Hot Rod Crowd" and "Gang Sweetheart."

One of the most unusual love comics to come out of that period is "Hearts and Flowers," done by Kirby for the December 1958/January 1959 issue of *Young Romance*. Kirby breaks the first law of love comics by having the **BOY** narrate the story. Keemo, handsome and moody in a turtleneck sweater, finds his pal Starky making unwelcome advances to the new girl in town, Dolly Fraser. Starky wears a loud plaid jacket and a cigarette dangles from his smirking lip, thus signifying that he's bad. Dolly, on the other hand, is a nice girl, as we can tell from her neat ponytail and simple clothes. Keemo rescues Dolly

"Hot Rod Crowd," from **Young Romance**, December 1950. Art by Simon and Kirby.

("Take off, Starky!") and sees her safely home. She invites him in, pours him coffee, and turns on the record player. "The music that came out was square as a frame," narrates the hard-boiled dialogue. "But it was moody and it washed over me like the waters of a dark ocean…" Keemo even meets Dolly's honest, upstanding folks.

But Keemo can't stay away from the mean streets ("On our street a guy was always alone—it was him against all the rest"), and there he runs into two pals, the usual cigarettes dangling from their mouths. They say, "Hi Keemo! You hear about Chita and Sugar Man?" Chita, it turns out, is Keemo's steady girl. He tracks her down to Sherman's drugstore, where she is sharing a most undelinquent banana split with Sugar Man. Sugar Man has—you guessed it—a cigarette dangling from the corner of his mouth. As for Chita, she wears an enormous flower in her long, curly hair—a sign that she is not a so-called nice girl. Keemo drags her outside. "You told me yesterday you were going out with some girlfriends today!" he accuses, and she responds (with what we are somehow sure

Jailbirds in love. "Doorway to Heartbreak," from **Personal Love**, July 1953, and "Lost Embrace," from **Sweethearts**, January 1949.

**MY CONFESSION**

SORRY, MISS TANNER, BUT WE CAN'T EMPLOY YOU... AFTER ALL, WITH YOUR REPUTATION... SORRY, I DIDN'T MEAN TO LET THAT SLIP OUT!

IS EVERYONE GOING TO HOLD ONE SLIP AGAINST ME ALL MY LIFE?!

"My Tarnished Reputation," from **My Confession**, October 1949. Art by Wallace Wood.

is a Spanish accent), "So I told you a lie! All the time I must try to make you jealous to get any attention!" He shuts her mouth with a passionate kiss and the caption reads, "Sure it would be a gal like Dolly Fraser I should marry one day…But I'm stuck with Chita because I love her." In a reversal of the expected ending, the tough guy and his tough gal walk off together into the night.

Sometimes in stories like "Lost Embrace," "Doorway to Heartbreak," "Discovered!" and "This Is My Punishment!" the tough kids even wind up in prison. After she's served her time, the girl tries to start a new life, only to fall for a nice guy. Afraid he'll find out her terrible secret, she rejects him and instead starts dating the man with the pencil-thin mustache. Every love comic reader knew what that meant—

# the guy was no good.

Sure enough, he tries to drag the heroine back into a life of crime, but at the last minute she changes her mind, turns him in to the law, and goes back to Mr. Nice Guy, who, it turns out, knew all along about her shameful past and didn't care.

In "My Tarnished Reputation," from *My Confession*, October 1949, the girl earns her bad rep by taking the fall for her embezzling boyfriend. The heroine of "I Was Unwanted," from the same issue, has it even worse. When she was eight years old, her mother killed her father and then committed suicide. Now she has no friends. "She's Marilyn Burke—her mother zzzzzz we don't have anything to do with her!" whispers a boy. Don't worry, though. Marilyn eventually grows up and meets a man who loves her despite her crazed killer mother.

"My Tarnished Reputation" and "I Was Unwanted" were both drawn by Wallace Wood, best known for his exquisite science-fiction and fantasy art in comic books like *Weird Science* and *Weird Fantasy*, published by horror-comics specialists EC Comics. Before their famous horror comics, even EC had attempted romance. *A Moon, A Girl... Romance* had started as a superheroine comic called *Moon Girl*. Just as Timely's superheroine title *Venus* changed genres in midstream, *Moon Girl* became a love comic in 1949, lasted a year, and by issue no. 13 had segued into *Weird Fantasy*.

The art in love comics ran the gamut from the seriously bad to the absolutely gorgeous. A really good love comic artist had to excel at drawing beautiful women, their large eyes framed with thick lashes and luminous with tears. Wood was one of the best artists, and another was Matt Baker, who

specialized in delineating lovely, stylish women. Today any comic with his name on the credits comes with a hefty price tag. Other artists were good, but displayed odd quirks. Ann Brewster, one of a small number of women drawing love comics, had the unusual habit of drawing all of her heroines exactly alike, so that it seemed as though the same woman was a "Flashy Blonde," "The Shy Type," and "Jealous"!

Once the war had ended and the boys came home and got their jobs back, there weren't many women left drawing comics. The few who stayed, like Ruth Atkinson, *Patsy Walker*'s early artist, drew love comics. Because artists tend to draw best what has interested them from childhood, women have rarely excelled in superhero action stories, but the romance genre suited them well. Even the most clichéd stories gave them an opportunity to draw handsome men and beautiful women in fashionable evening gowns.

By the sixties, even *Patsy Walker* and *Millie the Model* had become soap operas, and the two heroines spent much of that decade in tears. From 1961 to 1963, they were joined by the equally sudsy *Linda Carter, Student Nurse*. These and *Kathy*, another teen comic, made up Marvel's much diminished girls' comics. Stan Lee had discovered that college students liked his new line of superheroes, and was putting his creative energies into *Spiderman* and *The Fantastic Four*.

The *Archie* comics line, like the Energizer's pink bunny, was still going strong, and adding significant new titles. In October 1962, Sabrina the Teenage Witch, a co-creation of Dan DeCarlo and writer George Gladir, made her first appearance in *Archie's Mad House*, and a year later *Josie and the Pussycats* started, although at first the comic was simply called *She's Josie*, and the Pussycats would not become a rock group until 1970. Dan DeCarlo, who had been employed by Archie Publications for only a year, named Josie

Top and middle: **Millie the Model** and **Patsy Walker** turn sudsy in ads from 1965; bottom: **Linda Carter, Student Nurse**, 1962. Art by Al Hartley.

Opposite: A gallery of romance heroines, all drawn by Ann Brewster in 1957.

An ad for the greatly reduced girls' line of comics published by Marvel in 1962. Art by Stan Goldberg. Stan Lee wrote the ad as well as the comics.

The first Sabrina, in 1962, written by George Gladir and drawn by Dan DeCarlo.

Josie and the Pussycats, April 1970.

after his wife, and gave her the same bouffant hairdo. Sabrina would not get her own book until 1971, and by then both she and Josie starred in their own Saturday morning TV animated cartoons, along with Archie himself. As for Archie, having already had a hit radio show and a long-lasting newspaper strip, the only thing left for him was to form a rock-and-roll group, which he did. The Archies defined bubblegum music with their top-ten hit *Sugar, Sugar* in 1969. It should come as no surprise that during this time, *Archie* was the best-selling comic in the country.

By the end of the 1950s, the majority of comic-book publishers were gone, victims of the great comic-industry slump, and by the 1960s only Charlton, Marvel, and DC Comics were still publishing romances. Of the three, Charlton's were probably the absolute worst love comics ever produced. Each issue gave the impression that, after having blown their entire monthly budget on a beautiful cover, the editors parceled out the interior pages for peanuts to various talented high school student relatives of the staff. On top of the bad art, Charlton used mechanical lettering, which contributed a chilliness to their pages. DC Comics, all through the fifties and well into the sixties, also suffered from the cold. Unlike Charlton, DC's artists were faultless, but their style was mechanical and angular, perhaps better suited to the re-emerging superhero milieu. Marvel's romance comics were drawn in a friendlier style, with fetching, lush-lipped heroines, but by the sixties, both Marvel and DC's love comics had acquired that generic "pop art" look seen today on hundreds of campy T-shirts, cups, greeting cards, and Roy Lichtenstein paintings.

The entire country had changed drastically by the mid-sixties, and the surviving love comics tried to keep up with the change. Their heroines moved up in the world; they evolved from waitresses and housewives into college students, stewardesses, and rock stars. Love comic publishers attempted to sell more copies of their books by putting Elvis and the Beatles on the covers. Student protest became a theme ("How Can I Love a Member of the Establishment?"), and the heroine of "My Lover, My Enemy," from the July 1971 *Girls' Romances*, was even a counterspy. Unfortunately, the stories, no matter how well-drawn, read as though they were written by clueless forty-five-year-old men—which they were. The few women who had worked on love comics in the fifties were long gone. A desperate attempt to be hip in stories like "His Hair Is Long and I Love Him!" or

# "But How Could I Love a Square?"

resulted in such dialogue as "He's strictly dreamsville!", "Grow up! You're **YESTERDAY,** baby!", and "You're beautiful people, hon…and I sure dig your groove!"

The few surviving teen titles were equally unsuccessful as they tried to cash in on the new rock and roll and the hippie movement. Charlton came up

Rock and roll comes to romance comics: **Teen Confessions** and **I Love You**, January 1966; **Girls' Romances**, June 1965. (And isn't that Ann-Margret on the cover?)

"How Can I Love a Member of the Establishment?" written by Stan Lee (don't you believe that "as narrated to" stuff!), from **Young Romance**, a British reprint of Marvel romance comics circa 1970. Art by Don Heck and John Verpoorten.

"My Lover, My Enemy!" from **Girls' Romances**, July 1971.

with *Go-Go* in 1966, which featured badly drawn comics and photos of the Beatles and David McCallum (it was gone-gone in a year). Western Publishing's *The Modniks* was worse. Despite deserving a prize for most embarrassing pseudo-hip dialogue ever written ("Hi, big dad! Diggin' the sun?", "Tansville, man!"), it managed to last an amazing three years, from 1967 to 1970. In 1966, DC Comics came up with their take on mod, scooter-riding British rock stars with *Swing with Scooter*, a comic about a mod, scooter-riding British rock star. The art by Joe Orlando was clever and innovative, the writing ("Go, go, go! Frug, baby! Swing!") was dismal. And in the 1970s, DC published two comics, *Binky* and *Debbie's Dates*, that were far more than mere *Archie* wanna-bes—they were *Archie* clones. They were drawn precisely in the Archie style, with characters who looked exactly like the Archie characters: blond and brunette girls who were the spitting image of Betty and Veronica, even a high school principal who was the identical twin of Mr. Weatherbee. DC should have been ashamed.

One perfect teen comic did emerge in 1961, and it lasted an entire decade. *Thirteen, Going on Eighteen* was the creation of John Stanley, *Little Lulu*'s brilliant writer and artist. Drawing in a different style than he used for

Archie clones from DC. Opposite: from **Debbi's Dates**, July 1970. (Not Mr. Weatherbee and Reggie!) Above: from **Binky**, May 1971. (Not Betty and Veronica!)

Rock and roll comes to teen comics: **Go-Go**, August 1966; **The Modniks**, 1970; **Swing with Scooter**, July 1966. Scooter's art by Joe Orlando.

*Lulu* (where he was, of course, really copying Marge Henderson's style), Stanley chronicled the hilarious adventures of thirteen-year-old, ponytailed Val, her best friend Judy, and the boy next door, Val's sort-of boyfriend, Billy. John Stanley never embarrassed himself or his readers by trying to make his characters sound "hip"; instead, he wrote and drew stories that were every bit as clever as *Lulu*'s had been. In a 1964 story, Val sleepwalks through the streets of her town until a car horn wakes her up and she finds herself downtown, barefoot and in a quilted bathrobe, surrounded by a staring crowd. She races back home, praying, "Please, **PLEASE** don't let me meet anyone I **KNOW!**", and of course runs right into her brand-new boyfriend, Paul, walking with his mother. What's worse, Paul pretends not to know her and walks right by. Val arrives at her front door in tears, telling herself, "I'll bet **BILLY** wouldn't have pretended he didn't know me..." She passes two kids playing in front of her house, and one kid tells the other, "Look! That lady isn't wearing **SHOES!**"

**Thirteen, Going on Eighteen**, January 1966. Art and story by John Stanley.

Brokenhearted, Val lies down on her sofa and cries herself to sleep. A phone call from Paul wakes her up. "I'm surprised you have the nerve to call," yells Val. "**DON'T** pretend you didn't pretend you didn't know me on the street today..." Paul answers, "What are you **TALKING** about, Val? I haven't been out of the house **ALL DAY!**"

Val is delirious with joy ("The **WHOLE THING** was a dream from **BEGINNING** to **END!** I never left the house **AT ALL!**"), and she dresses up to go out. As she leaves the house, singing to herself, the same two kids are still playing outside. One says to

the other, "Look! That lady is wearing **SHOES** now!"

One perfect gem of a love comic also emerged from the sixties. *Mod Love*, published in 1967 by Western Publishing, had only a single issue, yet it's the most unusual and, along with the Simon and Kirby romances, the best love comic ever produced. *Mod Love* is sized larger than the average comic book and is printed on slick white paper instead of the usual yellowish newsprint. All three stories in the book are brilliantly illustrated by the same uncredited artist, in bright, complementary colors that pay homage to pop artist Peter Max and the Beatles film *Yellow Submarine*. On the back cover, George Harrison, in his Sergeant Pepper jacket, peers out from the window of a London bus. The stories, credited to Michael Lutin, are sophisticated and very mod. Heroines like Space Girl ("Half teenybopper—half vampire—**HER** orbit starts at sundown—") from "She's the Hippest Girl in the World" resemble 1960s supermodels Peggy Moffet and Jean Shrimpton. They find, and lose, and find again their musician lovers against backdrops of London, Venice, Rome, and Paris. Even the ads are unusual, and read as though they are also written by Michael Lutin. Instead of advertising a real commercial product, the ad on the inside front cover, telling the reader to "Drop away the *Ugly Fat*," turns out to be a new-age statement: "Do you have to **STARVE TO DEATH? NO.** You've got more sugar

Pages from the only issue of **Mod Love**, 1967. Above left: "She's the Hippest Girl in the World"; above right: "As Long As I Win."

"Beauty on a Budget," a fashion spread from **Young Love**, March 1977. Art by Elizabeth Berube.

stored up inside then you've ever dreamed. Make up your mind …there is **NOTHING TO SEND FOR…NOTHING TO BUY.** "And he means it!

With the dawn of the seventies, DC Comics made a last-ditch attempt to keep their shrinking love comics audience. They hired new, younger artists, including Elizabeth Berube, probably the last woman to draw for love comics, who contributed charming neo-retro–style pages of fashion and beauty tips. They featured stories with themes more in keeping with the new morality of the times: unwed mothers, prostitutes (but they never used the word), and lesbians (but God forbid they should use the word!). They even used the word *brassiere*, not used in comics since Patsy Walker had mentioned it fifteen years earlier.

They also, from 1971 to 1972, combined gothic mysteries with romance and came up with a title that didn't miss a beat: *The Sinister House of Secret Love*. Each issue was a complete gothic novel in comic form. In "The Bride of the Falcon," written by Frank Robbins and illustrated by Alex Toth and Frank Giacoia for issue no. 3, Kathy Harwood, young, blond, and American, flies to Venice, where Count Lorenzo DiFalco waits at Castel DiFalco on Isola Tranquillo to make her his bride. After a first gondolier flatly refuses to row her to the island ("The word 'tranquillo' means 'peaceful', si…but it also means…**DEAD!**"), she finds another gondolier, who reluctantly takes her there. She finally meets in person the darkly handsome count, whom she had hitherto met only in the personals column of a magazine, and his mother, the contessa ("…the ravaged appearance of a once-beautiful woman…"), in a wheelchair since her last stroke, and unable to speak. ("She gets worse every day, despite the efforts of Europe's best doctors!") Alas, Lorenzo must have his mother's approval to marry Kathy, and it's obvious that she's not about to give it. Lorenzo, his cape flying romantically behind him and his pet falcon perched on his shoulder, hints that only when his mother dies will they be able to marry. Soon, too, he shows his "other side"—one of "Sadistic...arrogant cruel-ty!"—when he slaps his servant and yells, "**SILENCE,** peasant! Speak only when you're spoken to!"

Roberto, the handsome second gondolier, shows up on the island briefly, just long enough to tell Kathy, "You...you **TRUSTING** little fool! Lorenzo will **NEVER** marry you! Not while **'SHE'** lives! He **CAN'T!** Even if he **WANTS** to...Because, you love-blind innocent—she's his..."

That's as far as Roberto gets before Lorenzo's falcon attacks him ("Strike, my pet...**STRIKE!!!**"), sending him into the water and certain death. ("The law is on my side! Let the mainland authorities find him!") Of course, Roberto returns, quite alive, announces that he is an agent of interpol and reveals that the contessa is not Lorenzo's mother—she is his wife, whom he has been slowly poisoning. The count and contessa go to their deaths together, off a cliff, and Kathy sails away from "the high fog-shrouded Isola Tranquillo" in the strong arms of the interpol agent. "Awaiting me," reads the caption, "was a future bright with hope and with love...."

But for all DC's last-minute flurry of creativity, it was a case of too lit-tle, too late. From 1961 to 1963, romance comics were still one of the top two genres of comic books on the newsstands. But from 1964 onward, that list is dominated by superhero comics. And as superheroes returned, romance went out the door. Over at Marvel, the last *Patsy Walker* comic was published in 1967. *Millie the Model* switched back to a funny format, drawn by Stan Goldberg in the same style as Dan DeCarlo, and made it to 1975. A year later, they published their last love comic. Charlton also canceled their love comics line in 1976.

Back at DC, the last issue of *Young Romance* came out in 1977. The first love title to be published had survived for thirty years. As far as the mainstream publishers were concerned, boys were back in and girls were out.

But for dozens of talented young women countrywide, what the main-stream thought didn't matter. They had already discovered that if you don't like the comics being produced, you can make your own. Sisters were doing it for themselves.

# Chapter Three

# Womyn's Comix

## 1970–1989

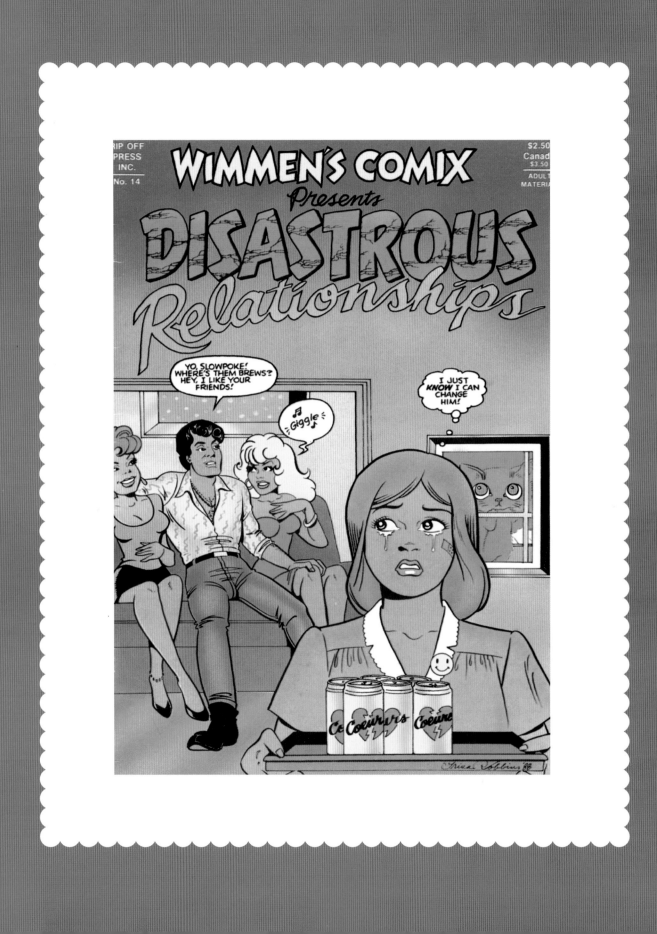

**IF THE** surviving mainstream teen and romance comics were clueless about the lifestyles of the 1960s and 1970s, they were at their most embarrassingly clueless in their attempts to deal with the new feminism, or what was then called "women's liberation." Stan Lee, who is credited with writing "No Man Is My Master" for a Marvel Comics romance book in the early 1970s, seems afraid to even call it women's liberation in the story. Instead he refers to "female freedom," fearing, perhaps, that the name is copyrighted, and he will be sued.

The story itself is a laugh and a half. Bev is dating Nick, who makes the term *sexist pig* sound like a compliment. He orders for her in restaurants ("I ordered you the roast duckling baby." "But I don't like roast duckling, Nick!" "Then it's time you learned to like it, Bev. My chick's gotta like what I like."), and then drags her to a boxing match. She thinks, "Nick is so groovy—if only he wouldn't be so bossy."

But when she objects, he tells her, "Chicks are **WEAK** little creatures. But they're **SOFT** and **CUDDLY**—and **BEAUTIFUL**—" Then Bev's girlfriend takes her to a "Female Freedom" rally. At the rally, "Suddenly my eyes were **OPEN**. I began to see things **DIFFERENTLY**." Bev thinks, "I'm **THROUGH** letting boys like **NICK HOWARD** put me down." Then she starts dating a bunch of complete wimps. "Before you go **IN**—" stutters one, standing in her doorway after a date, "I wondered if—that is—I mean—would you **MIND** if—?" Bev, who is definitely one brick short of a load, muses, "I thought I wanted a boy I could **DOMINATE**—a boy who would be no stronger than **I**. Well, gal, maybe that's what **SOME** females want—but I'm not one of them." Finally she gets Nick back, and in the last-panel clinch, he says, "**ME** Tarzan—**YOU** Jane! And **THAT'S** the way it was **MEANT** to be!" They deserve each other.

In "Miss Peeping Tom," from the May 1973 *Young Romance*, Tina is rejected when she tries to join her school's all-male camera club. "Photography's a **MAN'S** field!" says one boy. Another adds, "All girls are good for is **KNIT-TIN'** an' **NECKIN'!**" Her friend Wendy threatens the school principal, "If Tina won't be allowed to join the camera club only because she's a girl—Women's Lib might picket the school!" Obviously, the writer of this story believed, like Stan Lee may have, that there was an official, dues-paying organization called Women's Lib.

**Love and Romance**, March 1975.

Tina tries to join the camera club in "Miss Peeping Tom," from **Young Romance**, May 1973.

"No Man Is My Master!" Cover of a British reprint of Marvel love comics circa 1970.

The writer of "Call Me Ms," from Charlton's March 1975 *Love and Romance*, doesn't get it either. "I wouldn't be caught in the love-trap and give up my career as my mother had done when she married dad!" reads the caption. "No, I guess I was what they called a *Woman's Libber . . .*"

But by the clinch in the last panel, the heroine thinks, "I'll keep my job...but my marriage will always come first!"

Meanwhile, the real women's liberation movement was changing the lives of real women. Interestingly, the growth of the feminist movement paralleled that of the new underground comics movement. In 1963, the year Betty Friedan's groundbreaking book *The Feminine Mystique* was published, young cartoonists like Gilbert Shelton, Jack Jackson, and Frank Stack were already producing the first of what would soon be called underground comix. Just as Friedan challenged women's traditional roles as housewife and mother, Jackson and Stack challenged traditional American middle-class values with their satires "God Nose" and "The Adventures of Jesus," while Shelton parodied superheroes with his hilarious "Wonder Warthog." In 1966, the year of

the formation of the National Organization for Women (NOW), Joel Beck had already come out with his self-published comic book *Lenny of Laredo*, and weekly or monthly tabloids called underground newspapers, most of them featuring comics, sprang up throughout the country. West Coast papers included the *Berkeley Barb*, *Open City*, and the *LA Free Press*, while the major New York underground paper was *The East Village Other (EVO)*. I was an art school dropout in Los Angeles when I saw my first copy of *EVO* and was inspired by the comics inside to eventually move to New York and to produce my own comic strips. Coincidentally (or not), the comic that most inspired me was a psychedelically decorative strip called "Gentles Tripout," signed by Panzika. Two years passed before I discovered that Panzika was a woman, Nancy Kalish. But with that exception, underground comics in the 1960s were an almost exclusively male field.

By 1970, the women's liberation movement had grown substantial enough to be noticed and reported upon, if not necessarily understood, by the mass media. Headlines from major newspapers read, "Gals Unbutton Their Lib" and

# "Bra-Blitzed!"

Sadly, most of the male underground cartoonists understood as little about the new women's movement as the newspapers did, and reacted to what they perceived as a threat by drawing comix filled with graphic violence directed mostly at women. People—especially women people—who criticized this misogyny were not especially welcome in this alternative version of the old boys' club, and were not invited into the comix being produced.

Despite the general male antipathy, 1970 saw an explosion of feminist underground newspapers all over America. They had names like *Tooth and Nail*, *Everywoman*, *Ain't I A Woman?*, *Off Our Backs*, and *Goodbye To All That*. Many lasted only a few issues, though *Off Our Backs* is still being published. The San Francisco Bay Area was a steaming hotbed of feminism, and that year *It Ain't Me, Babe*, the first women's liberation newspaper in America, formed in Berkeley. By the second issue, I had found a place with the paper, drawing covers and comic strips for them.

Nancy Kalish (pseudonyms: Panzika, Hurricane Nancy) psychedelic page from **It Ain't Me, Babe**, 1970.

Aside from its Dylan-esque title, *It Ain't Me, Babe* reflected the anarchistic, counterculture rock-and-roll world of both underground comix and second-wave feminism. No last names were listed on the masthead, and, in fact, there was no official editor or art director. Every three weeks the *It Ain't Me, Babe* collective got together and, often with the aid of controlled substances, laid out the whole paper, hit or miss. This resulted in some pretty odd, but always creative, pages. And because the paper came out every three weeks, even though it only lasted for one intense year, it had more than twenty issues.

On the paper's back pages, I chronicled the not particularly subtle misadventures of a typical pre-liberation "Everywoman" I named Belinda Berkeley. Poor Belinda had gone through college only to end up working in an office (and doing all the cooking and housework) to support her pretentious and unliberated husband, Buzz, while he wrote the Great American Sex Novel. Issue by issue, the strip tackled the problems facing women in 1970, from oppressive advertising on television ("You've come a long way, baby!") and harassment on the street to the sexism of the New Left. Each episode was also a step toward Belinda's eventual liberation, which starts when her old college friend, Sandy Francisco, comes for dinner and fans Belinda's embers of resentment into the flames of revolution. "So I've gotten involved in women's liberation," she says, "…done great things for my head! Delicious dinner, Belinda…does Buzz ever cook?" She goes on, "Good grief, Buzz, you must be putting me on!

Belinda Berkeley walks down the street in **It Ain't Me, Babe** comix, 1970. Art and story by Trina Robbins.

"A Flower Fable," by Lisa Lyons, from **It Ain't Me, Babe** comix, 1970.

You mean you're actually writing porn? You were so radical back in school…don't you think you're sorta copping out?" Finally she ends, "…so we had this great speaker on the myth of the vaginal orgasm…please don't get up to do the dishes, Belinda! Buzz should do 'em if you cooked!" By the time Sandy leaves, Buzz is quite unhappy, and Belinda is primed for liberation.

Later that year, working with the newspaper collective, I got together the few women cartoonists I could find and produced the very first all-women comic, also called *It Ain't Me, Babe*, subtitled "Women's Liberation."

Like its namesake paper, the comic was of uneven quality, as were the majority of underground comix then. The diverse contents included a psychedelic comic by Willy Mendes, my strip about the Goddess, a sweetly political two-pager by Lisa Lyons, and caustic comments about enslaved office workers by Michele Brand. In the center was a comic strip, again written collectively, in which Juliet Jones, Daisy Duck, Supergirl, and other characters rebel against their sexist boyfriends. Just as women all over America were doing at the time, they form a consciousness-raising group. Petunia Pig says, "Now I see how I've been kept powerless all these years. Being married to Porky kept me isolated from other women. He was able to define my total reality." And Supergirl adds, "I've always felt I was better than other women because of my super powers and always preferred the company of men. How I was kidding myself! Men have never thought of me as an equal."

**Pandora's Box**, 1973. The Peters sisters discover that one of their friends is a lesbian. Art and story by Lyn Chevely.

In 1972, two separate groups of California women cartoonists came up with the same idea independently, each unaware of the other's existence. In Laguna Beach, Joyce Farmer and Lyn Chevely (using the pseudonym "Chin Lyvely"), two single-mother artists, reacted against the sexist treatment of women in underground comix by deciding to produce a comic that would deal with real female sexuality. They formed their own publishing company, Nanny Goat Productions, and came up with the outrageous title *Tits 'n' Clits*, featuring the adventures of those "perfectly permeable Peters sisters: Glinda, Wanda, and Fonda," and Mary Multipary, who became, in later issues, Mary Nullipary. The stories were indeed about sex from a woman's point of view—they dealt with such topics as vibrators, menstruation, IUDs, and men who miss the toilet bowl.

*Tits 'n' Clits* was the second all-women comic book and the first continuing all-women anthology. It lasted a healthy fifteen years, although in 1973, when the owners of the Laguna Beach bookstore that sold it—ironically called Fahrenheit 451—were arrested for selling pornography, Farmer and

Chevely changed the name for one issue to *Pandora's Box*. By the time *Pandora's Box* came out in 1973, it carried an ad on its inside back cover for thirteen other feminist underground comix, thereby launching the heyday of women's comics.

One of the best and most horrifying story lines produced by Farmer and Chevely, "The American Dream," ran in *Pandora's Box*. Sensitively drawn by Farmer, it's the feminist's answer to all those love comics that ended with a romantic wedding and a promise of "happily ever after." "The American Dream" is the story of Suzanne, who gave up her promising career as a poet to become the perfect wife, hostess, mother, and gourmet cook. Her not exactly supportive husband ("That was all **RIGHT!** Next time, though, please add a bit more sage to the game hen stuffing!") doesn't satisfy her sexually or emotionally, and she's too busy meeting the demands of him and her children to write anymore. The story builds in intensity as Suzanne gets more overwhelmed. At the breaking point, she tries reaching out to her husband ("Jonathan, I'd like to have some time alone with you…listen to music or something?"), but when he cancels out in favor of his job—*she*, of course, has given up *her* career—leaving her alone with three screaming kids for the weekend, she plans a dramatic and frightening suicide.

The same year that they published *Pandora's Box*, Farmer and Chevely produced one of the most important and underappreciated comic books to come out of the 1970s, *Abortion Eve*. Abortion had just been legalized countrywide. Farmer and Chevely, who were counselors at a women's free clinic, saw the need for a comic that explained abortion clearly and in a way that actually made good reading. With graceful art by Farmer, *Abortion Eve* tells the story of five pregnant Eves who meet at an abortion clinic—Evelyn, the suburban matron; Eva, the flower child; Evie, a troubled teenager; Eve, a feisty, savvy black woman; and Evita, an equally feisty Hispanic woman. They each have a different reason for wanting an abortion: neither Eve nor Evita can afford to add more children to their family, and

Suzanne ends "The American Dream" with a particularly frightening method of suicide, from **Pandora's Box**, 1973. Art and story by Joyce Farmer.

"Can This Marriage Be Saved?" from **Wimmen's Comix** no.1, 1972. Art and story by Shelby Sampson.

The four Eves discuss the merits of giving birth over abortion, from **Abortion Eve**, 1973. Art by Joyce Farmer.

Evelyn is pregnant with the child of her lover, not her husband, Adam. Poor Eva is simply too much of a space case to be a mother. In the course of the book, their counselor, Mary Multipary, explains to them, and to the reader, the choices they may have in abortion and in birth control, the legality of abortion, and what to expect during the procedure. On one page, Eve spouts off informatively, "Those old men on the supreme court finally found out what's been goin' on all the time—and they made a law to cover it!—almost—" She continues, "But I get **MAD** when they control my body by their laws!…Bring in a woman, an' if the problem is below her belly button and it ain't her appendix, man— you got judges an' lawyers an' priests an' assorted graybeards sniffin' an' fussin' an' tellin' that woman **WHAT** she gonna do an' **HOW** she gonna do it!"

At the same time that Farmer and Chevely were putting together their groundbreaking book, ten women cartoonists gathered in San Francisco to form the Wimmen's Comix Collective. The result of their meeting, *Wimmen's Comix*, arrived at comic-book stores three weeks after *Tits 'n' Clits*. In just two years since the publication of *It Ain't Me, Babe*, there were now enough women cartoonists to put out two different women's underground comix.

Like *Abortion Eve*, the first issue of Wimmen's Comix contained an abortion story, "A Teenage Abortion," by Lora Fountain, along with a sarcastic piece on sexism in the workplace by Lee Marrs and a story about pot and revolution by Sharon Rudahl. If you were part of the counterculture in the early 1970s, pot and revolution were your life. It was a time of communes and collectives, and, not unlike the production process of *It Ain't Me, Babe*, every issue of *Wimmen's Comix* was edited by two women, with much input from a core of contributors. But the results weren't always political. As the years and issues progressed, Lee Marrs drew a satire on every gothic romance ever written, Caryn Leschen produced a page on the toilets of Europe, Dori Seda did stories about her dog, and Melinda Gebbie contributed page after claustrophobic page about her sexual confusion.

    *Wimmen's Comix* no. 1 also contained the first autobiographical comic ever published, drawn by Aline Kominsky. Autobiography has since become a staple of comics drawn by women, and big chunks of women's comix

Three covers from **Wimmen's Comix**. Left to right: Lee Marrs, 1974; Lee Marrs, 1984; Shary Flenniken, 1975.

tend to be about the artist's dysfunctional family, miserable childhood, fat thighs, and boyfriend problems. Although Kominsky seems to have invented the form, the autobiographical comic actually harkens back to the confessional style of mainstream romance comics. Women do love to share confidences!

    My contribution to *Wimmen's Comix* no. 1 was "Sandy Comes Out," the first comic about a lesbian. In Portland, a young art student named Mary

Wings read "Sandy Comes Out," and waxed indignant about what she felt was a heterosexual take on lesbianism. Twenty-three years later, she wrote about her reaction for *Gay Comix*:

"The year was 1973. I was a sculpture major in art school. The anti-war movement had led me to feminism, and feminism—the concept—led me to lesbianism, the practice. It was a lot less theoretical than it sounds. One day, tired from a night of leafleting and tribadism, thumbing through a *Wimmen's Comix* I came upon Trina Robbins' story 'Sandy Comes Out.' I remember feeling alienated and angry…What about struggle, oppression, and the patriarchy? (Dig it, girls, we still live in a patriarchy.) Straight women are oppressing me all over the place—with their male identification and their nipples. Not to mention their boyfriends who—they mention—want to watch."

Wings decided, "I'll write *Come Out Comix* and tell it like it is." *Come Out Comix*, self-published by Wings on an offset press, was the first lesbian comic book ever produced. Wings followed it up with *Dyke Shorts* in 1978, and a drug awareness book, *Are Your Highs Getting You Down?*, which she produced in 1979 on a California Arts Council grant. Not content to rest on her laurels, Wings went on to write, in 1985, the first lesbian detective novel, *She Came Too Late*. Since then she has produced five books starring her lesbian sleuth, Emma Victor, plus a metaphysical mystery, *Divine Victim*.

In Southern California, Roberta Gregory also noticed the rampant heterosexuality of the first *Wimmen's Comix*, and reacted by drawing "A Modern Romance," which appeared in *Wimmen's* two years later. By 1976, Gregory had self-published her own solo comic, *Dynamite Damsels*, the first of a long, varied line of comic books she continues to produce.

Being published in *Wimmen's Comix* encouraged women cartoonists to go on and pro-

About this panel I drew, from "Sandy Comes Out" (**Wimmen's Comix** no.1, 1972), Mary Wings commented: "How can Trina make fun of this intrinsically poignant and metaphysical moment?"

"Working for the Aliens," from **Comix Book**, 1973. Art and story by Sharon Rudahl.

**Come Out Comix**, 1973. Art by Mary Wings.

duce their own comic books. Some who did so were Sharon Rudahl, Aline Kominsky, Melinda Gebbie, and Dori Seda. Being published in *It Ain't Me, Babe* had given me the courage I needed, and before the first *Wimmen's Comix* hit the stands, I had already put together *All Girl Thrills*, along with Willy Mendes and one Jewelie Goodvibes (remember, this was 1971!), and my own *Girl Fight* comics, while Mendes had produced the psychedelic *Illuminations*.

Feminists at that time were not exactly crazy about the use of the word *girl* in my titles. The new thinking was that *girl* was a demeaning term, just as boy had been a demeaning term for black men. I was attempting irony in my use of that word, but I didn't realize that I was about twenty years too early. In fact, *Wimmen's Comix* was criticized for keeping the word *men* in its title. Feminists were experimenting with new ways to spell their gender, such as *womon* or *womyn*.

A year after the first *Wimmen's Comix*, Lee Marrs came out with *Pudge, Girl Blimp*, a series that lasted through the decade. Pudge was a chronicle of the 1970s in Berkeley, and Marrs's busy, *Mad Comics*–inspired style turned it into a tossed salad of women's groups, communes, Patty Hearst, sex, drugs, and rock and roll. Into this mixture came Pudge, fat as her name implies, seventeen years old, and still a virgin. The little runaway from Normal, Illinois, dressed in a fringed jacket and frayed bellbottoms, is a far cry from

Willy Mendes's psychedelic cover to her book **Illuminations**, 1971.

Patsy Walker. "Gee whiz!" she exclaims, wandering blissfully through a crowd of rioting demonstrators, Hare Krishnas, and serial killers, "San Francisco! Enlightenment! Dope! Getting laid! Far out!" Everyone who had come to San Francisco since the Summer of Love, with flowers in their hair, could righteously dig it.

*It Ain't Me, Babe*, *Wimmen's Comix*, and the first issue of *Pudge, Girl Blimp* were all published by Last Gasp, a major San Francisco publisher of underground comix. In 1976, Denis Kitchen, a longtime underground cartoonist himself, and president of Kitchen Sink, a midwestern underground comix company, saw how well women's comics were selling, and asked me to put together a women's anthology comic for his company. I didn't want to resurrect *It Ain't Me, Babe*, and *Wimmen's* already existed as a feminist anthology, but, I realized, male cartoonists had been dealing with their often warped views of sex in their comics for a decade. Perhaps it was time for women to explore our own eroticism on the comics page. The result was *Wet Satin*, subtitled "Women's Erotic Fantasies."

*Wet Satin* provided an exhilarating experience for the women who worked on it, giggling as they drew. For a book with a single theme (sex),

Roberta Gregory explains her relationship with comics in **Click, Becoming Feminist**, 1977. Edited by Lynn Crosby.

**Pudge, Girl Blimp**, 1975. Art by Lee Marrs.

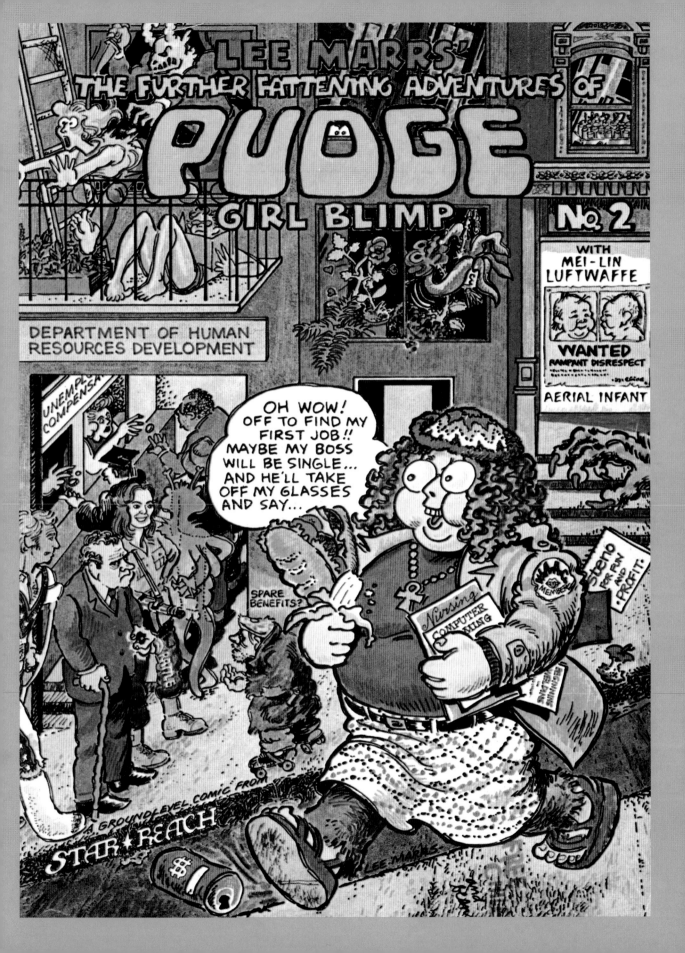

the stories were amazingly varied, from Lee Marrs's outdoorsy fantasies with
sexy anthropomorphic birds and animals to Melinda Gebbie's nightmare of a
beautiful epileptic in Charendon, a madhouse, during the French Revolution.
Joey Epstein even beat Lorena Bobbit to the punch by twenty years with her
cutting satire "Nifty Ways to Cleave Your Lover":

*"Slash it with a knife, wife!*
*Cut it with a scissors, sisters!*
*Strap it to a bomb, mom!*
*Use a broken glass, Cass!*
*Or a guillotine, Jean!"*

Melinda Gebbie's heroine of the French Revolution in **Wet Satin**, 1976.

Back cover of **Dynamite Damsels**, 1996. Art by Roberta Gregory.

The book almost immediately ran into trouble. Kitchen's midwestern printer took one look at the book, declared it pornographic, and flatly refused to touch it. This was interesting, considering that the same printer had printed an all-male sex book published by Kitchen featuring such an obscene cover it had to be covered with plain white paper before it could even be distributed to the comic stores. The printer insisted that the male sex book, *Bizarre Sex*, was satire, while *Wet Satin* was serious and therefore objectionable. Yet the underground sex newspaper *Screw*, hardly a feminist journal, said in a review, "The humor in *Wet Satin* is another welcome change from other undergrounds…What might have been a tedious and boring look into the sexual psyche of 'liberated' women turns out to be a series of clever, satirical, and entertaining cartoon strips."

*Wet Satin* finally got printed in the sexually liberal San Francisco, but when we had to go through the same problem with the second issue, putting out a comic about women's sexuality became too much of an uphill battle, and the second issue was its last.

A result of the 1960s sexual liberation was the unstable 1970s family structure. People lived communally, monogamy was often considered "bourgeois," and few marriages lasted. I was a single parent, as were most of the

A sadly prophetic page from Dori Seda's solo book, **Lonely Nights**, 1986. Seda died of emphysema two years later, at the age of thirty-six.

*FOR BACKGROUND ON S.O.T.V., SEE WIMMEN'S #13. **THIS DUBIOUS STATISTIC WAS ACTUALLY REPORTED IN ONE OF THE U.S.A.'S BOUGIE NEWSIES TO SCARE '80s SPINSTERS!

mothers I knew. In 1978, inspired by the way *Abortion Eve* had managed to entertain while educating, I put together *Mama! Dramas*, with eight other women cartoonists who were also mothers, most of them single mothers. Our goal was to show the kind of motherhood that didn't exist in *The Ladies Home Journal.* We drew stories about communal living, alternative schools,

"Mom," **Mama! Dramas**, 1978. Art and story by Suzy Varty.

playgroups, single parenting, and the realities of being on welfare.

   Delores Thom's 1978 story "**LEISURELY** Welfare Living" demonstrates to the 1990s reader that "welfare reform" is not a new concept. Mary is hardly the welfare queen made famous in Republican mythology. Her husband has left her, and she's stuck: "David's got the job, the training, the credit… Let's see who wants to hire an ex-housewife!" But the only work she qualifies for, as a checker in a supermarket, won't even cover essentials like child care and medical bills. (Child support as an alternative to dead-end jobs isn't even

"New Age, Same Old Shit!," **Wimmen's Comix**, 1989. Art and story by Angela Bocage.

Cover of **After Shock**, 1981. Art by Rebecca Wilson.

mentioned in Thom's story. It was just as impossible to collect then as it is now.) Mary applies for welfare. The caseworker gives her a hard time, and her kids recite the anti-welfare myths they've picked up at school: "Sally's mom's on welfare, and some kid at school says she eats out of his dad's pocket!" The grand sum of $356 a month doesn't go far. Her kids beg, "Mama, I wanna take dance lessons," and "Star Wars! Mama please." Her answer: "We can't afford it." Her house is sold, and she and her ex-husband split the equity, which isn't enough to buy another home. She applies for a loan to buy a new house, of course is turned down, and is "economically forced to live in the ghetto." Her caseworker continues to give her a hard time. By the last panel, Mary's check is late, she's out of food, and she stands hunched over the phone, crying, as her caseworker yells at her: "I don't like people like you. You just don't appreciate what you're getting!!"

On the positive side, Joyce Farmer shows that not all single mothers are doomed to a life of misery. Her back cover depicts a cozy suburban kitchen, lace curtains blowing in the breeze. A briefcase full of files, lying open on a kitchen chair, shows that the African-American single mother who lives here is a successful businesswoman. And sure enough, as her kids romp on the floor with the family cats, she hands her little old mother a sheaf of bills. "Glad to help, mamma!" she says, "And there's more where that came from!"

Then the 1980s arrived. Ronald Reagan, who did more to popularize the myth of the welfare queen than anyone, was elected president, and the mood of the country changed, almost overnight. In scores of subtle ways, women were urged back into traditional roles of wives and mothers. The media announced that feminism was dead, and that an unmarried woman over thirty had a better chance of getting killed by terrorists than of getting married. The term *politically correct* became a negative buzzword, and the term *postfeminist* was created to describe a new generation of women who, like heroines in the old love comics, found their fulfillment in a home and husband. Mona Charen, in the *National Review*, personified the postfeminist when she wrote that the women's movement "has effectively robbed us of one thing upon which the happiness of most women rests—men."

By 1985, even the Wimmen's Comix Collective had fallen for the hype and boasted of a "politically incorrect" issue. Editor Diane Noomin, in the 1991 anthology *Twisted Sisters*, proudly identified the original *Twisted Sisters* underground comic book that she and Aline Kominsky had put out in 1976 as "politically incorrect." Symbolic of the antifeminist backlash was *After Shock*, an all-woman underground comix anthology published in 1981. Editor Rebecca Wilson set the tone of the book with her cover, on which a chic woman, more robot than human, sits, sipping coffee on an elegant sofa. Next to her on the table stands her biological clock, which reads one minute to midnight. All around her, atomic explosions and tsunamis destroy the world, while in the background, the baby she never got around to having weeps, "Mommy??" The book stresses that the only way to cure women's dysfunctional lives is for them to have babies. Marian Kester's introduction tells us, "Civilization wants to commit suicide. So what starts to happen is: we're made to feel like **NOT REPRODUCING**. This can take the form of a horror of pregnancy… or annoyance at the idea of sacrificing yourself for some ungrateful little brat, or 'economic' considerations like

# 'How could I afford kids on my salary?'"

The editorial, by Wilson, dedicates the book to "the three children conceived and born to contributing artists during the year of its production."

All was not lost. Gay cartoonist Howard Cruse started *Gay Comix* in 1980. This book, the first gay comic anthology, published and continues to publish many of the best lesbian cartoonists, like Jennifer Camper, Joan Hilty, and

Two stories with a similar theme from **Gay Comix**.

Left: art and story by Mary Wings, 1980; right: art and story by Jackie Urbanovic and "Bird," 1983.

Cheela Smith. After four issues, Robert Triptow took over as editor for the remainder of the 1980s, and Andy Mangels has edited it since 1991. When Mangels took over *Gay Comix*, he made the decision to always include an equal number of pages by women and men, and the book continues to be one of the top showcases for both established and new lesbian cartoonists.

**Split-Level Dykes To Watch Out For**, 1998. Art and story by Alison Bechdel.

One of the most well-known lesbian cartoonists featured in *Gay Comix* was Alison Bechdel, who started at a New York women's newspaper, *Womanews*, in 1983. Within two years, she was self-syndicating her strip "Dykes to Watch Out For" in gay and lesbian papers across the country. By 1986, her strips were collected into the first of a series of books published by Firebrand Books, which continue to come out regularly. Bechdel's fame is well deserved. Her characters are real, and funny as only real people can be. Some are butch, some are not; some have babies, some don't; some shave their legs, and some don't. Reading her stories is more fun than watching any TV sitcom.

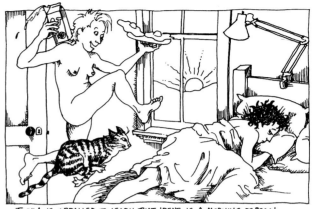

TWYLA IS APPALLED TO LEARN THAT IRENE IS A MORNING PERSON.

Alison Bechdel, 1984.

By the mid-1980s, it had been almost a decade since the publication of the last mainstream comic for girls. Only the unsinkable *Archie* remained for girls to read. Romance comics were long gone but fondly remembered. The classic love comic–style drawing of a woman, tear in her eye, agonizing over *something*—a lost love, a lost job, the baby she forgot to have—appeared on T-shirts, cups, cards, and in advertising…everywhere but in comic books. And some women cartoonists missed the girl comics of their youth enough to attempt, with varying degrees of success, to revive them.

Archie's pals 'n' gals, still going strong in 1984. Art by Dan DeCarlo.

In 1985, Barb Rausch and *Katy Keene*–creator Bill Woggon produced *Vicki Valentine* for independent publisher Deni Loubert. It was a contemporary rerun of Woggon's old *Katy Keene* comics, down to the reader-designed clothes and paper dolls. Woggon even made guest appearances in the book, dressed in his familiar cowboy getup, as "Wild Bill Hiccup."

**Vicki Valentine** no.1, 1985. Story by Bill Woggon, art by Barb Rausch.

Colleen Doran's beautiful Beardsley-esque tubercular heroine, "Eugene," from **Renegade Romance** no.2, 1988.

In 1986, I managed to convince Marvel Comics to give teen comics another try with my six-part series *Meet Misty*, and when that ended I produced
*California Girls*, an eight-part teen series, for the independent publisher
Eclipse. At the same time, Barbara Slate had talked DC Comics into publishing
her girl comic *Angel Love*. Although all these books received enthusiastic mail
from comic-hungry girls across the country, none lasted over a year. Loubert
and I even made a brief attempt to bring back a more contemporary version
of love comics in 1987, when I edited two issues of *Renegade Romance* for

Three attempts to revive girls' comics in the 1980s. Left to right: Trina Robbins, **Meet Misty**, 1986;
Barbara Slate, **Angel Love**, 1986; Trina Robbins, **California Girls**, 1987.

her company, Renegade Press. But it had been too long since women and girls
had bought comics. Comic shops, the only places to buy comics in the 1980s,
were filled with superhero comics, and had become the sole province of boys.

But love comics had not completely disappeared. In 1982, Gilbert and
Jaime Hernandez introduced *Love and Rockets*, a new kind of love comic for

Cynthia Martin's gothic romance "Nöe," from **Renegade Romance** no.1, 1987.

grown-up girls. While their books have always had a large male readership, they also have a uniquely female appeal. Gilbert Hernandez's series *Heartbreak Soup* is, in fact, reminiscent of that female favorite, the soap opera. He relates the continuing saga of Palomar, a small town described as "somewhere below the US border," and the stories of the men, women, and children who live there, especially the women. These memorable characters include Chelo, the woman sheriff; the radical Tonantzin, who dresses like her namesake pre-Columbian goddess as a political statement; and especially Luba, a woman who is large-breasted but never a "babe," with powerful Indian features that reflect her inner strength.

Gilbert Hernandez's unforgettable Luba, from **Love and Rockets**. Above left: as a teenager; above right: as a matriarch.

Jaime Hernandez, drawing in a crisp, Dan DeCarlo–inspired style, shares the book with his brother. His characters are as human as any comic characters can be. Since her initial appearance, his not-quite-twentysomething protagonist, Maggie, has added poundage to her thighs, hips, and rear, the way women really do, making her the first comic character to gain weight realistically. Young women readers, who graduated from Betty and Veronica to Maggie and her best friend Hopy, are attracted to Jaime's sympathetic chronicles of the cute punk-rock girlfriends and their cute punk-rock pals 'n' gals. *Love and Rockets* is a Riot Grrrl comic, created before the term was invented.

Jaime Hernandez's cute punk-rock pals 'n' gals, from **Love and Rockets**, 1987.

# Chapter Four

# Grrrlz' Comix

## THE 1990s

IN 1992, *Wimmen's Comix* finally removed the word men from its name and became *Wimmin's Comix*. By then, though, it no longer mattered. Young women had started to reclaim the word girl, just as the gay movement had reclaimed the word queer, and they were using the previously forbidden word in the titles of their comics: *Real Girl, Action Girl, Deep Girl, Girl Hero, Girltalk, Girljock, Rude Girls and Dangerous Women*. (It's interesting to note here that throughout the 1990s, "bad girl" comics—the kind produced for adolescent and teenaged boys, and starring hypersexualized women with large breasts and little clothing—are often preceded by the word lady, as in *Lady Death, Lady Justice*, and *Lady Rawhide*, while the feminist comics have the word girl in their titles.)

*Real Girl*, the first of the "girl" comics, started with the new decade, in 1990. Editor Angela Bocage subtitled it "The Sex Comik for All Genders and Orientations by Artists Who Are Good in Bed." True to its title, *Real Girl* features artists of both genders, and emphasizes comics that deal with every variation of sex, positive and negative: abortion, harassment, AIDS, lesbians, cross-dressers, and paper dolls of people like Gertrude Stein and Alice B. Toklas or Valerie Solanis, author of the *SCUM Manifesto* and would-be assassin of Andy Warhol.

In an article in Real Girl no. 1, Rebecka Wright defines girl as opposed to woman:

"Perhaps you're wondering why *Real Girl*? Why not *Real Woman*? Isn't "girl" a patronizing term for an adult female? Listen, junior, while it's true that this form of address is best reserved for intimates, some of the best people around call themselves girls. Quite a few call *themselves* women. The twain often meet, even in the same person, but there are some philosophical differences.

"Sex, just to choose an example at random, has certain, well, serious and lasting connotations for women that just don't apply to girls. A 'fallen woman' is ruined; a 'bad girl' is only naughty….

"Not that it's all a game for girls, but there don't seem to be quite so many lurking consequences for them. There is a certain amount of freedom of action accorded adult girls, as succinctly put by this popular bumpersticker:

# Good girls go to heaven.

Times had changed, and that feminist warhorse *Wimmin's Comix*, after going through three publishers and twenty years, put out its last issue in 1992. Past issues had highlighted such themes as men, little girls, and work—there had even been a 3-D issue—but this last one was the "kvetch issue." In her editorial kvetch, Caryn Leschen echoed the frustrations of too many women cartoonists while explaining why there would be no more issues of the longest-lasting women's anthology comic:

"This book has been printed on cheap paper which will turn yellow in a

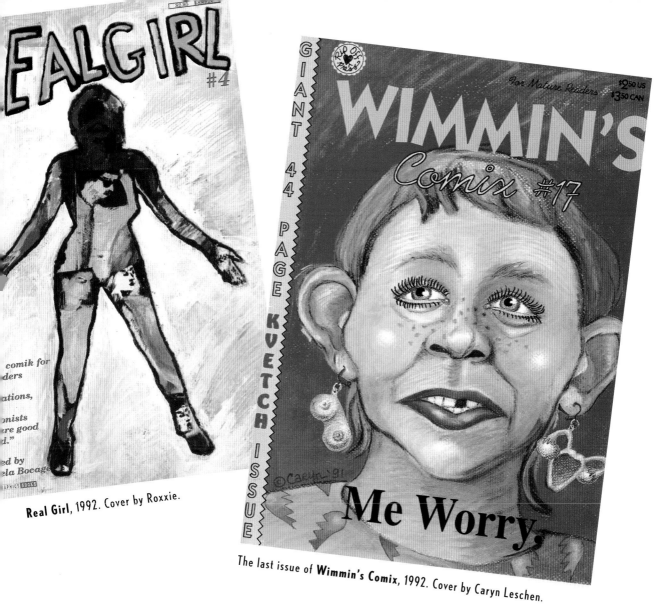

Real Girl, 1992. Cover by Roxxie.

The last issue of **Wimmin's Comix**, 1992. Cover by Caryn Leschen.

# Bad girls go everywhere."

few years. The print run was too small and all the stores, as usual, will sell out, but they won't reorder because 'Women don't buy comix.' Bullshit. How did they sell out in the first place? It's always like that. What a waste of time and energy. Forget it."

After the close of their longtime home at *Wimmin's Comix*, some cartoonists moved on to *Twisted Sisters*, under the editorship of Diane Noomin. *Twisted Sisters*, which began as a two-issue comic book in the 1970s, was revived in 1991 as a book, collecting earlier work by fourteen women cartoonists, much of it from *Wimmin's Comix*. After that, Noomin edited four more issues as a comic book, expanded to include the work of newer, younger women cartoonists. And there were definitely enough to choose from; throughout the 1990s, scads of women cartoonists emerged on the pages of anthologies and their own comic books. *Twisted Sisters* exemplifies the tendencies of contemporary women cartoonists to produce autobiographical stories. Issue no. 3, from 1994, is typical; of four stories in the book, three are literally "true confessions." The main difference between these and the earlier love comics is that *Twisted Sisters'* confessions all deal with sex: the high school girl protagonist of Debbie Drechsler's "Sixteen" is raped; in Caryn Leschen's "Dutch Treat," a bride honeymooning in Europe sleeps with an old boyfriend; and Phoebe Gloeckner spins the unsettling tale of a fifteen-year-old runaway in a world of bad drugs and worse sex.

"Nina's Wonderful World of P.M.S.", from **Wimmin's Comix**, 1992. Art and story by Nina Paley.

Like the old love comics, these stories are narrated in first person, but in the case of *Twisted Sisters*, we believe them to be true. Unlike the old love comics, with their tacked-on happy endings, many of the newer women's comic autobiographies range from mildly to extremely depressing.

But it's not all true confessions for the women who produce girl comics; they share a strong political and feminist awareness that they're not ashamed to talk about, and none of them are likely to boast of being politically incorrect. Many of the women in *Girltalk* also contributed to *World War 3*, an unapologetically radical comic book put together by a collective of both

**Action Girl**, 1997. Cover by Tavisha Wolfgarth.

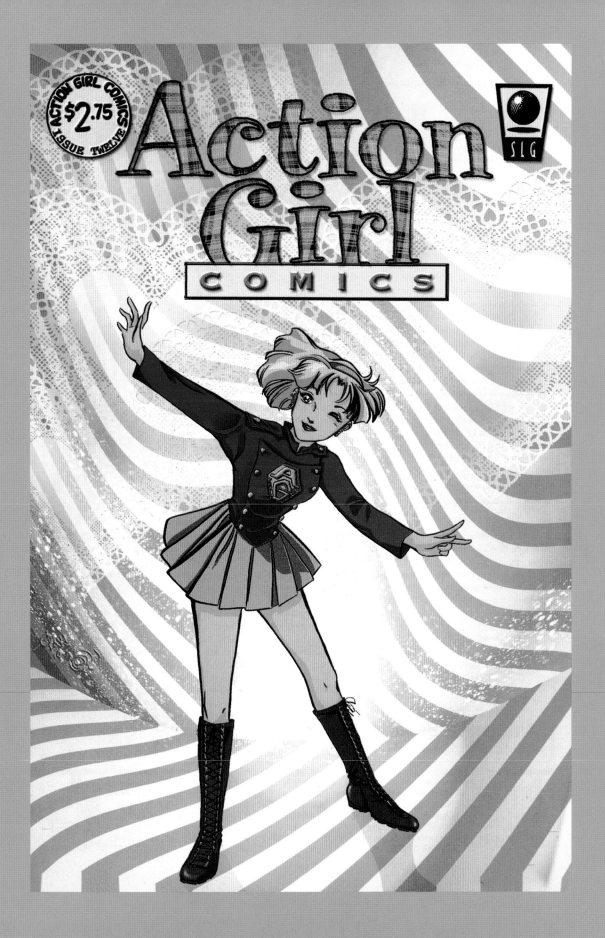

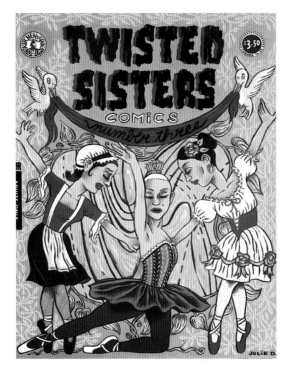

**Twisted Sisters**. Cover by Julie Doucet.

"Minnie's 3rd Love," from **Twisted Sisters**, 1994. Art and story by Phoebe Gloeckner.

male and female New York artists. In their 1992 special issue on sexism, Sabrina Jones wrote:

"Today most women expect to enjoy certain hard-won rights of the feminist movement, while disavowing feminism itself. They're afraid to alienate the men in their lives, who still hold most of the power. The male-dominated editorial board of *World War 3* considers itself variously leftist/radical/progressive/anarchist…and therefore open to feminism. In spite of these good intentions, the few feminist pieces we accepted just didn't seem to fit in."

The editorial board's answer, Jones continues, was to produce a special issue on sexism, but she has her doubts: "The material will be ghettoized—men won't read it, and then when we get more work on the topic, you'll say, 'We already covered that.'" *Girltalk*, which started three years later, would seem to have been the answer to Jones's problem. The editors define girl talk as "a safer haven that can handle anything from delirium to despair." But not all the

"Sixteen," from **Twisted Sisters**, 1994. Art and story by Debbie Drechsler.

**Girltalk**, 1995. Cover by Ann Decker.

**Girl Hero**, 1994. Paper doll cover by Megan Kelso.

contributors are women. One of the more powerful pieces in issue no. 2 is "Six Single Mothers," by Lance Tooks. His grim parody of a child's rhyme starts: "One single mother/ Rougher side of town/ had to take a second job/ To keep expenses down/ Can't afford a safer street/ Living in a dive/ Came home late one Friday night/ Then there were five." The last verse is the most tragic: "One forgotten mother/ Bare and callused feet/ Paid her taxes regular/ And wound up on the street/ Fought so hard to fix her life/ Until they took her son/ Strain turned out to be too much/ Then there were none."

Some of the girl heroes in Megan Kelso's comic book, *Girl Hero*, are Animata, Bottlecap, and Yolanda, three superpowered factory workers fomenting revolution against the corporate rulers of a near-future dystopia. But

**Slutburger**, 1992. Cover by
Mary Fleener.

**Dirty Plotte**, 1997. Cover
by Julie Doucet.

**Deep Girl**, 1994. Cover by
Ariel Bordeaux.

**Saucy Li'l Tart**, 1996.
Cover by Molly Kiely.

**Girljock**, 1995. Cover by
Trina Robbins.

**Naughty Bits**, 1991, with
cover girl Bitchy Bitch. Art
by Roberta Gregory.

despite the often grim messages in her book, Kelso includes paper dolls of her characters, a tradition left over from the girl comics of the forties.

Paper dolls are also a regular feature of *Action Girl*, an anthology comic book that combines feminism with an upbeat girls-just-wanna-have-fun attitude. In her editorials for *Action Girl* comics, Sarah Dyer describes her book's upbeat philosophy ("girl-positive and female-friendly—never anti-boy"), and proceeds to give the reader a political pep talk:

"Remember—**ACTION IS EVERYTHING!** Our society, even when it's trying to be 'alternative' usually just promotes a consumerist mentality. Buying things isn't evil, but if that's all you do, your life is pretty pointless.

Be an **ACTION GIRL** (or boy)!…go out and do something with all that positive energy!"

Merely reclaiming the word *girl* was not enough for some women cartoonists, who went still further, following the tradition of *Tits 'n' Clits*. These women reclaim some seriously objectionable words in comics like Mary Fleener's

A strip from **Action Girl**, 1995. Art and story by Patty Leidy.

*Slutburger*, Molly Kiely's *Saucy Li'l Tart*, the anthology *On Our Butts*, Roberta Gregory's *Naughty Bits* (starring Bitchy Bitch), and Julie Doucet's *Dirty Plotte* (*plotte* is French Canadian slang for a woman's naughty bits). Such in-your-face titles are a symbolic bird defiantly flipped at the reader. "Sure," says the artist, "I'm a slut, a bitch. *Je suis une plotte.* You got a problem with that?"

Other women cartoonists go to the opposite extreme and turn sweetness inside out. Dame Darcy (*Meatcake*) and Christine Shields (*Blue Hole*) might well be the love children of Edward Gorey and Drusilla, the vampire from the television cult favorite *Buffy the Vampire Slayer*. Their comic books are 100 percent girl, but with a dark twist: sugar and spice and arsenic, and antique dolls in bloodstained lace bonnets. On the pages of both books, girls in thrift shop dresses (I, for one, strongly suspect they resemble the artists), drift through disturbing, dreamlike Victorian universes. Darcy's main character is a girl named Richard Dirt, who, with her long blond hair and granny boots, looks like a warped Alice in

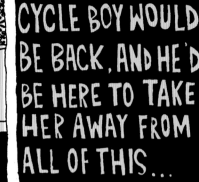

Panels from **On Our Butts**, 1994. Clockwise, from the top: "Motorcycle Boy," Fawn Gehweiler; Lisa Onomoto's gothic homage to Edward Gorey, "Little Goth Girl"; untitled by Anna Costa.

**Naughty Bits**, 1991. Roberta Gregory explains the creation of Bitchy Bitch.

Wonderland. She and her Siamese-twin girlfriends Hindrance and Perfidia look like little darlings from some fin de siècle photo album, but they guzzle their booze right from the bottle. In *Blue Hole*, Shields relates the true story of a tragic San Francisco double murder, carried out Romeo and Juliet style. Her heroine, Ruby, also takes her rotgut straight, and in the company of pirates, no less. Yet both comics are so darn cute! Except for the aforementioned Edward Gorey, it would be hard to imagine any man drawing comics like these.

If Christine Shields and Dame Darcy turn sweetness inside out, Linda Medley stands the Brothers Grimm on their heads with her self-published book, *Castle Waiting*. Drawing in the style of a classic fairy tale illustrator, Medley interweaves the frog prince, Rumplestiltskin, the Brementown musicians, and every other fairy tale our mothers lulled us to sleep with. The castle itself is Sleeping Beauty's old home, still surrounded by its brambly fence years after the princess departed with her prince, leaving the other inhabitants (including a curious bird-headed creature called Rackham, named after the great fantasy artist Arthur Rackham) waiting for travelers who have stories of their own.

**Blue Hole**, 1997. Art and story by Christine Shields.

The mosh pit experience from a girl's point of view. **Repressed in Portland,** 1996. Art and story by Mara Siciliano.

Still other women cartoonists use the word *girl*, but spell it with three Rs.

In the summer of 1991 a girls' movement was created in America with the odd merging of Washington, D.C., and Washington State. That was when two all-girl punk bands, Bikini Kill and Bratmobile, both from Olympia, Washington, came to D.C. for an extended stay. Our nation's capital had long been the scene of a flourishing punk movement, which was predominantly male. The few women in the punk scene were angry at the increasingly macho violence of the male punkers, which kept them out of the scene, sometimes with real physical threats. The result of their anger was a revival of feminism—1990s-style "third wave feminism."

**Meatcake,** 1997. Art and story by Dame Darcy.

Many of the young women, most in their teens and twenties, had been brought up in nonsexist and nontraditional ways by mothers who had themselves been part of the "second-wave feminism" of the 1970s. (The first wave is considered to be the early suffragettes.) The daughters of these women grew up understanding the concept of sexism, and taking for granted many of the gains made by that earlier movement. Along came the backlash, and young women found their security rudely shattered by threats to their reproductive rights, and by a new wave of sexism and homophobia. They were still not free to walk down the street without being harassed. They were mad as hell and they weren't going to take it.

The girls of Bikini Kill and Bratmobile got together, coming up with such slogans as "Revolution girls style now," and the term *Riot Grrrl*. Two of them, Allison Wolte and Molly Neuman, put together the first Riot Grrrl zine, using that name, and the movement was born. "Grrrl" combined that reclaimed word *girl* with a defiant growl—these were no well-mannered, pink-ribboned

"*nice girls.*"

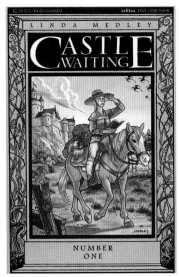

**Castle Waiting**, 1997. Cover by Linda Medley.

"Identity Crisis," from **Rude Girls and Dangerous Women**, 1994. Art and story by Jennifer Camper.

Within a year, the first Riot Grrrl convention took place in D.C., and chapters formed all over the country. As with the "Women's Lib" movement twenty years earlier, the national media was quick to cover it and slow to understand it. Riot Grrrlz were stereotyped as lesbians and/or violent man-haters. Actually, one of the first Riot Grrrl actions was to protest violence in a traditionally feminist collective way, by reclaiming the mosh pit, that crushing and frightening all-male area in front of the band at concerts. To make a space for themselves, the girls formed packs and forced their way to the front en masse, each protecting the other.

As much as the Riot Grrrl movement was about music, it was also about zines, self-published photocopied mini-magazines with print runs ranging anywhere from thirty to five hundred copies. Riot Grrrlz didn't invent fanzines, nor did the punk movement. The fanzine goes as far back as the early 1930s, when young science-fiction fans reproduced their own small magazines on messy mimeographs and even messier hectographs, crude precursors to today's more accessible photocopy machines. Many of the young fans who produced them eventually became professional writers and editors. The early zines, much as their later counterparts, were often letters in mini-magazine form, illustrated or not, featuring news and reviews of the latest science-fiction book or chatty personal information. And like today's zines, they could be traded for other zines or they were available through the mail for anything from a postage stamp to a couple of quarters.

The next group to utilize zines were comic fans in the early 1960s. Some of the earliest underground comix were hardly more than zines produced with only slightly more sophisticated printing equipment, and some of today's well-known comics professionals started in their pages. The advent of cheap photocopying in the 1980s liberated the zine. Anyone with something to say could afford to self-publish. By the 1990s, women, feeling the need to communicate with each other and empowered by Riot Grrrlz, adopted the zine as the perfect

medium in which to share their personal life stories, rants, philosophies, humor, poetry—and comics.

Like the early science-fiction and comic fans, some of today's well-known women cartoonists, like Diane DiMassa, Mary Fleener, Ariel Bordeaux, and Jessica Abel, started by publishing their own zines. Although their drawing styles are miles apart, both Abel's *Artbabe* and Bordeaux's *No Love Lost* (her zine was called *Deep Girl*) typify the mildly depressing autobiographical genre so often found in women's and grrrlz' zines and comics. Not much happens, and what does, happens in "real time." Girls agonize over boys, attend concerts, sit in cafes, discuss their relationships with their girlfriends. No real conclusions have been reached by the end of the book.

So many women's autobiographical comics are depressing, and so many are about dysfunctional families, that it becomes tempting to believe that dysfunctional families breed women cartoonists. Luckily, there is Ellen Forney. In her self-published comic, *I Was Seven in '75*, Forney tells a warm, upbeat story about growing up in the 1970s with hippie parents. Not that bad things don't happen in the stories— Forney's brother gets five stitches when

**No Love Lost**, 1997. Cover by Ariel Bordeaux.

he hits his head on a chair, the kids manage to set fire to their new microwave, and her parents survive a pot bust when the baby-sitter turns them in to the cops— but these are your average everyday bad things. No one gets abused, raped, or permanently robbed of their self-esteem by rotten parents. Forney's parents are, in fact, terrific; she and her brother are normal, happy kids. Her book is sweet, funny, and refreshing.

volume two, number one

mature readers $2.95/$3.95 (can)

artbabe

by jessica abel

FANTAGRAPHICS BOOKS

**Artbabe**, the comic book, 1997.

artbabe 4

$1.50

JESSICA ABEL ©1995

**Artbabe**, the zine, 1995. Cover by Jessica Abel.

Diane DiMassa's *Hot-head Paisan, Homicidal Lesbian Terrorist*, the angriest woman in comics since Bitchy Bitch, doesn't get depressed either—she acts, and acts violently. While Roberta Gregory's Bitchy Bitch (and her lesbian counterpart, Butchy Butch) is guaranteed to go postal several times in each issue of *Naughty Bits*, once the fit passes she's left as wretched as before. Hothead's rage, on the other hand, is cathartic—for the reader as well—and makes for some of the happiest violence you ever saw.

Hothead and Daphne, the girl she's madly in love with, sit on a park bench, happy together in the sunshine, when a huge man sits down next to them, spreading out his legs and invading their space the way huge men who spread their legs and invade your space have a way of doing. You gotta hand it to her, Hothead gives him a chance. She stares at the leg and says, "Uh, pardon me...," but the guy mutters, "Whatcher problem?" With a demonic grin, Hothead produces a hatchet out of nowhere, chops off the offending leg, and hands it to him. "This!" she announces. "This is my problem! Does this belong to you? Because if it does, I found it way over here in **MY** space!"

Hothead and Daphne go to the movies and a seriously tall dude, wearing a baseball cap, sits right in front of Hothead. Again, she gives him a chance first. "Yoo-hoo, Mr. Total eclipse of the sun . . .' she says. "You're twelve feet tall and you wear a hat to the movies? And ya sit in front? Why didn't ya wear a **COWBOY** hat??? Whatta gonna do next? Open up an **UMBREL-LA**??" Naturally, the tall guy ignores her and continues to sit, legs spread apart (of course), revealing the sentences, "Me a big boy, me have special rights" written on the crotch of his jeans. Again, Hothead grins maniacally and while Daphne applauds, produces a chain saw from thin air and saws the guy in half. "He was in my way," she explains, "I couldn't accept that."

Besides, Hothead has a really cute cat named Chicken, who wears a fez.

Zine art ranges from amazingly excellent to mondo scratcho, but the not-very-good artists don't care if their work is crude. They're simply following the advice Sarah Dyer gives in *Action Girl*: "Don't think you can do comics? Try anyway, even if it's just for yourself!" They're producing illustrated letters,

Roberta Gregory's Bitchy Bitch goes postal.

**I Was Seven in '75**, 1997. Art and story by Ellen Forney.

Hothead Paisan, 1994. Art by Diane DiMassa.

Chicken the cat receives his fez and loves it. **Hothead Paisan**, 1994. Art and story by Diane DiMassa.

not art galleries to be sent through the mail. As with letters, they share their days, their friends, and their fun with the reader.

In *Ducks in a Row*, Bonni Moeller fits lists of her friends' one hundred favorite things ("1. Beer, 2. The Ramones, 3. Good shoes, 4. Burritos…") between pages of delicately crosshatched comics. Carrie McNinch's art style is the complete opposite of Moeller's; she uses heavy, solid blacks and strong, woodcut-like outlines. But she's just as chatty. On the first page of *The Assassin and the Whiner* she shares with the reader her delight at finding the original ship used in *Gilligan's Island*, her favorite cooking show on PBS, her grandfather's funeral, her family's reaction to her coming out as a lesbian, her enjoyment of Ellen DeGeneres's "coming out episode," and her appreciation of the guy in her local comic-book store, who gives her discounts. In *Cone of Silence*, Kelly Renee shares with her readers "Men That Have

Made Me Feel Wanton," a list that includes her high school crush, her grade school dream boy, and The Fonz. Tina, one of three grrrlz who produce *Buffy and Jody's Guide to the Galaxy*, tells us about the best friends she had in school, and in another issue the girls (Tina, Ami, and Alexis; no last names supplied) supply the recipe for deep-fried spaghetti ("serve with garlic bread and cherry kool aide"). Beth Templeton plays on the 1970s desire to "share." She produces postcards that read, "Sure, I'll share," and her zines ask, "Want Some of My Insomnia?", "Want Some of the Crap I Carry Around?"

After all this cheerful sharing, the bite in the zines comes as a shock, until we remember that grrrl is part growl. Canadian zine artist Patti Kim writes letters on Hello Kitty stationary and peppers her zines with cute Japanese cartoon characters, but when you turn a page, you come to this declaration:

### "FIRST MOURN...THEN WORK FOR CHANGE...

On December 6, 1989, 14 women were murdered in Montreal. Women of every race and class are abused and killed by men they know. We mourn, and work for change..."

A gynecology lesson from **Maxine**, 1996. Art and story by Sari Wilson and Josh.

A gallery of zine art. Top row, left to right: **Ducks in a Row**, Bonni Moeller; **Want Some?**, Beth Templeton; **Ab Inspector**, Patti Kim; bottom row, left to right: Untitled comic by Carrie McNinch, from **Asswhine**; "Helga's Life," by Helga Romoser, from **Happy Hour**; "Mimi's Adventure in Wonderland," by Tina, from **Buffy and Jody's Guide to the Galaxy.**

One topic dealt with in a majority of zines is women's bodies, and our obsession with weight. Beth Templeton draws a comic about her breast reduction operation, commenting, "Why couldn't I be satisfied with my body? Why did one asshole doctor's controlled and surgically accepted violence on my body make such a difference?"

In *Cone of Silence*, Kelly Renee draws a disturbing comic about bulimia, "Living On Empty." As the bulimic waits in line at the supermarket to buy the junk food she'll devour, then throw up, "An image of the sainted Princess Diana sticking a lovely, manicured finger down her royal throat comes to mind. It is comforting. She would know. She would understand."

Following the comic is a parody of all those "Now You Are a Woman" pamphlets our mothers gave us, but instead of instructions on the use of sanitary napkins, it's a manual on how to be a bulimic. Some helpful tips: "Running water is an effective way to disguise sounds of gagging or retching." "Remember: you can learn to purge quietly!"

"My Amazing Secret," in *Buffy and Jody's Guide to the Galaxy*, provides another parody on weight loss, using copy from real ads: "*Suddenly—*

"The Magic of Spontaneous Combustion," from **Cone of Silence**, 1997. Kelly Renee finds another answer to the problem that plagued Hothead Paisan.

134

**Cuckoo**, 1997. The artist's "alters" come out for Christmas. Art and story by Madison Clell.

*for the first time in my life—I started to lose weight!!!!* It was a miracle! The fat seemed to just melt away. I *finally* discovered *the Secret* to losing weight! It was all so simple…so easy! So I just kept doing it. And I kept getting thinner and thinner." In Tina's accompanying art, the protagonist becomes a living skeleton. Finally, in the last panel, she reveals "the Secret"—a crack pipe, a lighter, and rocks of crack, with accompanying directions, "1. Put rock in pipe. 2. Light the pipe. 3. Smoke pipe."

Madison Clell and Kim Hecht put out the most serious zine of all, but even here, there's room for humor. *Cuckoo* is subtitled "One Woman's True Stories of Living with Multiple Personality Disorder." Madison Clell draws a delighted psychology major, pointing with pride at the "multiple" she's discovered—Clell herself, turned into a giant furry guinea pig. She calls this "Guinea Pig Syndrome." Sometimes ironic, sometimes dead serious, sometimes with rage, Clell, using an expressionistic brush style, introduces us to the

**Mystery Date**, 1997. This mini-comic had a print run of thirty! Art and story by Carla Speed McNeil.

**The Mysterious Tea Party**, 1997. Art and story by Kalah Allen.

different people, whom she calls "alters," sharing her body. One is eight-year-old Melanie, who was raped as a child. "There's a technical term for what was inflicted on Melanie," Clell writes. "Phrases for clarity in courtrooms and doctor's notes. Names to tame monstrous actions. Sodomy. Rape. Child molestation. **BULLSHIT!** Words can never describe the reality."

*Cuckoo* is not for kids or for those looking for a laugh. It's strong stuff, and it's important stuff.

Not much, actually, *is* out there for kids these days in the way of comics. The unsinkable *Archie* stands alone. *Pep*, the comic that started it all back in 1941, was finally canceled in 1989, but the *Archie* line is still going strong. In the 1990s, a character was added to Archie's crowd of pals and gals—Cheryl Blossom, a redhead who's twice as rich and three times as bitchy as Veronica—and in 1997, *Sabrina the Teenage Witch* became the latest in a long string of hit television series based on *Archie* characters. *Archie*'s only competition during the entire 1990s was *Barbie* comics, published by Marvel from 1990 through 1995. Currently, if little girls want to read a comic, their only choice is the *Archie* group.

**Archie** in the nineties. Top, left to right: Sabrina; Cheryl Blossom; bottom, left to right: Josie and the Pussycats; Betty and Veronica, same as they ever were.

Lovers' leap, from **Cathedral Child**, 1998. Art and story by Lea Hernandez.

Mainstream love comics have fared even worse. There *are* no mainstream love comics. However, the genre keeps getting revived by smaller publishers. Lea Hernandez combines romance with *manga*, the Japanese comic style, and a form of science fiction known as "steam punk," in her graphic novel *Cathedral Child*. Steam punk stories take place in some alternate past that has modern technology. Thus, Hernandez's story takes place in 1897; her heroine wears granny shoes, but she works with an *analytical engine*—their term for a computer.

All those old "nurses in love" comics are taken one step further by Jimmie Robinson in his comic-book sendup of the *ER*-style soaps, *Code Blue*. Jayeen "Chicken" Michaels is head of staff at Highland, a low-end, crumbling county hospital. In her words, "We handle the homeless, runaways, addicts, you name it." On an average day, Jayeen deals with emergencies ranging from a mad bomber to the hunky head doctor of pricey, high-tech Northridge Hospital on the other side of town. She helps subdue the bomber and saves the doctor's life when he's brought in after a traffic pileup. But when he tries to date her, she's too resentful to admit she likes him: "I'd hate to deprive that fancy chrome building of its head doctor. The thought of some middle-aged woman missing out on her tummy-tuck and hip-suck…it brings shivers down my spine." Readers wondering when the cute doctor will conquer Jayeen's foolish pride must wait for the next issue to find out.

The most traditionally campy romance comic of the 1990s is *Eternal Romance*, Janet Hetherington's blend of Roy Lichtenstein paintings and vampire stories. Perfectly parodying the traditional love comics style, Hetherington tells true confessions with a 1990s edge. In the first issue of her book, subtitled

**Barbie**, 1994. Story by Barbara Slate, art by Mary Wilshire and Trina Robbins. On this prophetic page, editor Hildy Mesnik (center) tells the **Barbie** crew that the comic has been canceled. In the story it turns out to be an April Fools' joke, but the book was canceled a year later.

**"*Love! Heartache! Vampires!*"** the romantic leads, like the love comics genre, refuse to stay dead. They are all vampires. In later issues, Hetherington widens her scope to include anyone good-looking and supernatural. The love interest in "Mummy's Boy" is obvious. In "Once Bitten, Twice Shy," Joey's ex-girlfriend, Rochelle, suddenly pops back into his life, much to the dismay of his current girlfriend, Joyce. When the two finally come to blows over him, Rochelle reveals she's a vampire, but they're evenly matched—Joyce is a witch.

"**NO!** sob! I **CAN NEVER** marry you!" sobs Lin, the heroine of "Kiss of Death," also in the third issue of *Eternal Romance.* "My family is…**CURSED!**" And indeed, one kiss transforms her into a rather cute werewolf. But it turns out that her fiancé is a werewolf, too, and the couple is free to howl at the moon together, happily ever after.

Doctors in love, from **Code Blue**, 1998. Art and story by Jimmie Robinson.

**Strangers in Paradise**, 1994. Francine explains the title. Art and story by Terry Moore.

A girl and her rat, from **The Tale of One Bad Rat**, 1995. Art and story by Bryan Talbot.

Obviously, men can create girl comics, too, as they have since the 1940s. Terry Moore's *Strangers in Paradise* is probably the best 1990s successor to *Love and Rockets*, which is no longer being published. Girls who once graduated from Betty and Veronica to Maggie and Hopy can now go straight to Francine and Katchoo. Moore's art is excellent, his stories moving and funny, his characters real. Like Maggie from *Love and Rockets*, Moore's pleasingly plump Francine proves that one doesn't have to be an anorexic supermodel to be absolutely adorable.

One of the best graphic novels of the 1990s, if not of the century, is Bryan Talbot's *The Tale of One Bad Rat*, a sensitive, beautifully drawn story of childhood sexual abuse. Helen, a teenage runaway, has fled from an abusive father and a cold, uncaring mother. As she begs on the streets of London, sleeping in alleys and abandoned buildings, her only companions are her pet rat and the Beatrix Potter books she has loved since childhood. When a cat kills her rat, Helen begins a pilgrimage to Beatrix Potter's home which will eventually lead to her own healing. The rat, which has become a kind of giant spirit guide visible only to her, accompanies Helen on her odyssey.

With all the wonderful girl comics out there, one would think that women and girls of all ages have all the comics they could want, and that the comics creators are in paradise, expressing themselves on paper and making a decent living doing so. This could not be further from the truth. The average woman cartoonist has a day job. Her books are hard to find. Zines, of course, are usually only available through the mail, but with few exceptions, even the better-selling girls' comics usually have a small print run compared to mainstream superhero comics, and very few comic-book stores bother to carry them. Beth Templeton describes the situation perfectly in *Want Some?*:

"These days when I stake out a comic-book store, I'm looking for comics by women, or local self-published things…It's not hard to find stores devoid of both. No 'Artbabe,' 'Hothead Paisan,' 'Dirty Plotte,' or 'Dykes to Watch Out For' but, they would be 'happy to order something in for you.' Uh, no thanks. If I can't browse from a great selection, how will I find anything new?"

The result, of course, is that comparatively few women even know these comics exist. To further compound the irony, self-published or small-press black-and-white comics are usually priced higher than mainstream, full-color superhero comics, yet women earn less than men, and have less buying power.

It's a sorry situation, and in 1993, women decided to do something about it. During the San Diego comics convention, a group of women who worked in comics met at a coffeehouse to discuss the problems of working in such a male-dominated industry. The result of the meeting was the formation of Friends of Lulu, a national organization named for the plucky little girl who never gave up on her attempts to crash the boys' club. Their stated purpose is "to promote and encourage female readership and participation in the comic book industry." In February 1997, Friends of Lulu held their first annual conference, and in August of that year, they honored women creators and women-friendly comic books at their first annual Lulu awards ceremony.

As we come to the close of the twentieth century, the comic industry, such a vital art and communication form for over sixty years, is in real trouble. In fact, the industry has never been in worse shape.

Comic-book sales are at their lowest in fifty years. There was a time when one in three periodicals sold in the United States was a comic book. *Walt Disney's Comics and Stories* sold over four million issues every month. Other titles, including some westerns, crime comics, and the Simon and Kirby romance comics, sold more than one million copies per issue. Ninety percent of the nation were regular comics readers. Today that number is less than 1 percent. In fact, if 1 percent of the population read comics today, the industry would be considered healthy. The average mainstream superhero comic sells from forty thousand to

Diane DiMassa's Hothead says it all. **Hothead Paisan**, 1994.

sixty thousand copies. (And, of course, the average mainstream comic book is always a superhero comic!) The average black-and-white, independently published comic book sells about three thousand copies.

This had all happened before, although not on such a disastrous scale, when superhero comics, the biggest sellers during World War II, lost their popularity after the war, and were replaced by other genres, including teen comics and love comics. Tastes change and pendulums swing. The pendulum, which swung back to superhero comics in the 1960s, has reversed itself again.

Comic-book editors, publishers, and retailers like to blame television for the decline in their field, but people have not stopped reading. A 1998 survey by *Publishers Weekly* found that readers were buying three times as many books as they had bought the year before. The survey also found that they're young, under thirty-five, and that 58 percent of them are women, as opposed to 42 percent men. Obviously, there are books out there—lots of them—that women want to read. Women make up 52 percent of the population, and they like to read. It doesn't take a rocket scientist to figure out that they would also like to read comics, if publishers would only produce comics for them to read.

The motto of Friends of Lulu is "Here To Save Comics." Once upon a time there was a woman named Ginger Rogers who could dance as well as Fred Astaire, only backwards and in high heels. If a woman could do that, saving comics ought to be a snap.

## *Afterword*

This is not a book about women cartoonists—I've already written that book—even though, for at least the past twenty-odd years, it's been women who have for the most part produced comics for women and girls. But some of the comics being produced by truly great women cartoonists today just don't fit my definition of girls' comics; while these cartoonists' books are certainly not aimed exclusively at men, they are gender neutral. I'd like to recommend them, just because I like their work so much: Carla Speed McNeil's *Finder* is quirky science fiction with a really cute guy hero; Erika Lopez writes real books, not comic books, but her cartoony *Flaming Iguanas* and *Lap Dancing for Mommy* are girl comics at their most wacko in book form; Donna Barr's *Desert Peach* defies definition. It's about General Rommel's (yes, the World War II German general!) fictional, gay, younger brother. Finally, enough cannot be said about *Mad Raccoons* by Cathy Hill. Her whimsical book, obviously inspired by the late Walt Kelly's *Pogo*, introduces such characters as Raccketty Ann, a sweet girl raccoon who resembles a certain famous stuffed doll, and Uncle Erf, who appears to have multiple personalities, including that of the family dog.

Look for these books. It doesn't have to be a girl comic to be a good comic.

# Index